NORTH-WESTERN EUROPEAN
LANGUAGE EVOLUTION
Supplement vol. 4

North-Western European Language Evolution (NOWELE) is a scholarly journal which publishes articles dealing with all aspects of the (pre-)histories of – and with intra- and extralinguistic factors contributing to change and variation within – Icelandic, Faroese, Norwegian, Swedish, Danish, Frisian, Dutch, German, English, Gothic and the early Runic language. *NOWELE* is edited by Erik W. Hansen & Hans F. Nielsen (Odense University) in collaboration with an international Editorial and Advisory Board.

Richard L. Morris

RUNIC AND MEDITERRANEAN EPIGRAPHY

John Benjamins Publishing Company

Amsterdam / Philadelphia

Acknowledgments

I would like to thank the following people and organizations whose help and support played a major role in the writing and production of *Runic and Mediterranean Epigraphy*. At the head of the list stands Professor Elmer Antonsen of the University of Illinois at Urbana-Champaign who more than anyone has given generously of his time and knowledge in discussing all aspects of my work. I would also like to thank Marie Stoklund, Director of the Runic-Epigraphic Laboratory at the National Museum in Copenhagen, for facilitating my access to inscriptions in the Museum's collections and for fruitful discussions. Others to whom I am indebted are Professors Marianne Kalinke of the Department of Germanic Languages and Literatures and Ladislav Zgusta of the Department of Classics at the University of Illinois at Urbana-Champaign for their support and advice.

Among the organizations I would like to thank are the American-Scandinavian Foundation in New York for awarding me the Henrik Kauffmann Fund Grant in 1984 which enabled me to travel to Copenhagen, examine inscriptions in the National Museum, and to use the Wimmer Collection at the Royal Library.

My thanks also to the following publishers and journals for permitting me to reproduce the following tables and illustrations: *Arkiv för nordisk filologi* for Otto von Friesen's summary of alphabet derivations (Table 1), Oxford University Press for Lillian Jeffery's table of archaic Greek letter forms (Table 2), Egbert Forsten Publishing for John Sandys's table of archaic Latin letters (Table 4), Manchester University Press for Ralph Elliott's table of attested medieval rune-names, to the Istituto Poligrafico e Zecca dello Stato for Margherita Guarducci's illustrations of Greek inscriptions (figs. 4, 5, 6, 7), and to the Deutsches Archäologisches Institut for Ernst Zinn's illustrations of writing directions (figs. 8, 9, 10, 11, 12).

Lastly my thanks go to Dr. Hans F. Nielsen of Odense Universitet for his assistance in the preparation and publication of *Runic and Mediterranean Epigraphy*.

Richard L. Morris

ISBN 978 87 7492 683 2   (Pb ; alk. paper)
ISBN 978 90 272 7291 1   (Eb)

John Benjamins Publishing Co. · P.O. Box 36224 · 1020 ME Amsterdam · The Netherlands
John Benjamins North America · P.O. Box 27519 · Philadelphia PA 19118-0519 · USA

CONTENTS

Contents

Contents

Contents

Contents

Contents

LIST OF TABLES

LIST OF FIGURES

0. INTRODUCTION

Since the 19th century, when scholars seriously began debating the origin of the runes, many theses have been put forward and remain to this day the subject of often heated debate. The opinions on the runes' origin, as well as on the time of their inception, differ widely. Already in the last century, Wimmer (1887:11) wrote:

> Die frage nach dem alter und dem ursprung der runen ist so oft aufgeworfen und auf so viele verschiedenen weisen beantwortet worden, dass man fast versucht sein könnte zu sagen, dass alle möglichen, denkbaren und undenkbaren ansichten zu worte gekommen sind. Man hat auf der einen seite die runen so alt gemacht wie die sündflut, auf der andern seite jünger als die einführung des christentums im norden; man hat sie sich von den nordischen völkern selbst ohne das vorbild irgend eines fremden alphabetes erfunden gedacht, und man hat sie von einer menge älterer und jüngerer alphabete abzuleiten gesucht. Es ist eine sehr grosse literatur, die hier vorliegt; aber die qualität steht leider im ungekehrten verhältnis zur quantität.

My purpose here shall not be to add yet another theory to the list of already existing ones. I hope to point out throughout the course of this investigation that we simply do not know with certainty where the runes come from and that we should keep an open mind concerning investigations which reevaluate the data and come to conclusions which do not agree with presently or formerly held beliefs. To assume a priori that the runes cannot be older than the birth of Christ, is not only based on insufficient evidence, but it also leads to fallacious interpretations of the inscriptions themselves.

1

0. Introduction

I intend to discuss the epigraphic features of the older runic inscriptions, not only to establish a runic tradition, but also to bring to light the many striking similarities which the runic tradition shares with the Mediterranean epigraphic traditions. I propose, however, to accomplish this by examining the Greek and Latin traditions in their preclassical stages, for this is the period in which a source for the runic tradition must be sought. Similarities between the runic writing system and the archaic Latin and Greek systems have heretofore been ignored or explained away as being the result of imperfect attempts by a primitive Germanic people to master epigraphic writing, because scholars sought to compare the runic tradition with the highly refined classical traditions of Imperial Rome and Hellenistic Greece. Strikingly different results are obtained when the runic tradition is juxtaposed to the Mediterranean traditions in their earlier stages of development. The aspects of epigraphy to be examined are the alphabets themselves, the phonological values of the letters, the direction of writing, the use of ligatures, interpunction, the vocabulary of writing, writing techniques, types of inscriptions, and spelling conventions.

0.1. On alphabet borrowing

Isaac Gelb (1963:201) believes that the development of writing in all cultures is subject to the principle of unidirectional development. He writes: 'What this principle means in the history of writing is that in reaching its ultimate development writing, whatever its forerunners may be, must pass through the stages of logography, syllabography, and alphabetography in this, and no other order. Therefore, no writing can start with a syllabic or alphabetic stage unless it is borrowed, directly or indirectly, from a system which has gone through all the previous stages'. The runes do comprise an alphabet. Of this there is no doubt. In light of Gelb's statement, then we must assume that the runes were borrowed from somewhere.

With the exception of the more radical German scholars in the

2

0.1. On alphabet borrowing

Third Reich (see now Hunger 1984), all serious modern students of the runes have recognized the fact that runic writing is derived from the great Mediterranean writing tradition. Their greatest efforts have been directed toward the identification of a particular Mediterranean alphabet as the source from which the runes were borrowed. Because this search for the mother alphabet has not resulted in definitive identification, recent research, particularly by Erik Moltke (following Fritz Askeberg), has sought to overcome the most obvious obstacles to an equation of the runic alphabet with the Latin alphabet by assuming that the borrowing was 'indirect', that runic writing was inspired by the Latin alphabet but was developed with considerable independence in a place (i.e. Denmark) remote enough from the Roman *limes* to make such an independent development plausible. With very few exceptions, the search for the origin of the runes has concentrated on establishing a one-to-one correspondence between the graphs of the supposed lending and receiving alphabets, sometimes with little or no attention given to the phonological values of these graphs and their phonological-orthographic fit in the different alphabets. Recent research has almost never taken into consideration the much broader question of the writing *systems* as a whole, which must include much more than the borrowing and adaptation of the individual graphs. Early attempts in the 19th century to consider this broader question were squelched by Ludvig Wimmer's contention that the striking similarities between the runic and archaic Mediterranean inscriptions are merely coincidental, conditioned by the primitive nature of both scripts. Wimmer's view seemed to be supported by the prevailing assumption concerning the date of the borrowing (or adaptation of the runic alphabet, usually placed in the early centuries after the birth of Christ.

An analogy might be drawn here between learning a foreign language and learning a foreign system. When a person learns a foreign language, he does not simply learn the lexicon. For his use of that foreign language to be effective, he must learn the entire system, not only the lexicon but also the syntax, the morphology, and the phonology. In addition to borrowing the individual letters of a foreign alphabet, the

3

0. Introduction

original user(s) of the runes surely also borrowed such other features as direction of writing, the interpuncts, ligatures, and other orthographic conventions that were part-and-parcel of the lending writing tradition. The borrowing process might not result in a perfect replica of the original, but we should expect to find traces of more than one feature from the lending tradition in the borrowing one. To this end, I will examine the runic writing *system* in light of the archaic Latin and Greek systems for traces of features which have not been pointed out in previous scholarship or which have been ignored.

Leonard Bloomfield (1933:201) makes the observation:

> The transfer of writing to a new language occurs, apparently, in this way, that some bilingual person who knows writing in one language, hits upon the notion of using the alphabet also for his other language. He may retain whatever defects the alphabet had in the first language and he may retain letters that are necessary in the first language but superfluous in the new one, and he may fail to devise new letters for additional phonemes of the new language. On the other hand, he or his successors may be clever enough to mend these defects, either by inventing new characters or by putting superfluous characters to good use, or by semiphonetic devices, such as using combinations of letters for a single phoneme.

The adoption of the Semitic alphabet by the Greeks provides an example for what Bloomfield has said. The Greeks derived their vowel letters from Semitic consonantal letters which were of little use to the Greeks in their Semitic values. Classicists apply this axiom without further ado. Few handbooks on the Greek alphabet fail to mention that Semitic *aleph* began with a glottal stop. Since this glottal stop was not phonemic in Greek, the Greeks adopted *aleph* with a vocalic value, hence *alpha*. Classical epigraphists, such as Lillian Jeffery (1961), assume that the Greeks who adopted the Semitic alphabet to the Greek language must have known how to speak and write a Semitic language.

4

0.1. On alphabet borrowing

Similarly, we must assume then that at least one Germanic-speaking person knew how to speak and to write the language of the people from whom he was borrowing the alphabet. If he, as well as other Germanic people, knew a foreign language, we can assume contact between the two language groups (see Lehman 1977). Archeological evidence of trading contacts between Scandinavia and the Mediterranean world exists already for the Bronze Age. I refer here to the amber trade routes (see Navarro 1925; Spekke 1957; Rice 1980).

No one in runic studies, to my knowledge, has ever explicitly pointed out that in order to adopt someone else's alphabet, directly or indirectly, the native learner must be able to communicate with the foreign teacher. I assume that the learner was a native speaker of Germanic because the runic alphabet fits the Germanic phonological system so well (see 4.3).

At this point, I drew on de Saussure's famous distinction between *langue* and *parole* and their interplay. The linguistic sign, *signum,* is understood because it is transmitted by speech, *signans,* and perceived by the listener, *signatum.* Once the listener has perceived the sign, he interprets it in his own mind and, in the best of all possible worlds, understands it as it was meant to be understood by the speaker. In order for the listener to understand the speaker, the listener must know the system of signs the speaker is using. A speaker of German and a speaker of English cannot communicate with each other unless one knows the sign system, i.e. language, of the other. If we extrapolate and say that the sign, in the case of alphabet borrowings, is an individual graph, which represents a phone, and apply this statement to the situation of the runes – remembering that writing is a secondary linguistic device – then we must try to imagine how a speaker of Germanic analyzed the sounds he heard when he was attempting to learn to write his own language. If person X of language Z said [ō] but the Germanic person did not have [ō] in his phoneme inventory, we must ask how the Germanic person analyzed [ō] in terms of his own language. If the graph § is associated with [ō] in language Z, then whatever value the Germanic person assigns to [ō] in his own inventory will be associated with the graph §.

5

0. Introduction

This analytic process necessarily implies that a Germanic speaker must have known how to speak and write a Mediterranean language before he could make the association between a Mediterranean graph and a sound in the Mediterranean language. Being able to write also implies that a person can analyze and separate sound sequences into distinctive segments and then graphically reproduce them. Judging from the phonemic character of the older fuþark (4.3), this Germanic speaker must have analyzed his language in the same fashion in which he learned to associate a particular sound in (for example) Greek with a particular Greek letter. This process is of course extremely complex and much more involved than simply seeing that someone else wrote and deciding that it would be a good idea to do the same for one's own language.

The situation is comparable to a field linguist attempting to devise a writing system for a language that has none. Before he can devise an alphabet system for a language, he must first be aware of the graphic-phonological correspondence indispensable for alphabet writing. This awareness presupposes that he knows how to write. Then he must make an analysis of the language to determine which phonological items require representation in order to produce an effective written image of the target language.

0.2. Exclusion of the Etruscan alphabet

I have excluded the Etruscan alphabets from consideration for phonological reasons. While the Etruscan alphabets may optically resemble the runes, the runes maintain the distinction between voiced and voiceless obstruents all too carefully. The Etruscan language had no voiced stops nor did the Etruscans employ the Greek graphs for those stops, although *beta, gamma,* and *delta* were retained in the Etruscan alphabet (Pfiffig 1969:26, 36-8). The same is true of /o/ in Etruscan (Pfiffig 1969:28-9). If the Etruscans had mediated an alphabet to the Germanic peoples, we would expect some confusion in the use of voiced versus voiceless stops in the runic inscriptions similar to the use of Lat. C for both c and g (3.1, 3.2).

0.3. Goals

This investigation will attempt to show that the questions, 'Where did the runes come from?', has not yet been answered because the features of the archaic Greek and Latin alphabets have not been given their due weight. In fact, this question, in all probability, can never be answered beyond a shadow of a doubt. The intercultural relationships in preclassical Europe were complex, which in turn makes the detection of cultural influences or exchanges complex. The purpose of this investigation is to demonstrate that a connection between the older runic alphabet and the archaic Greek and Latin alphabets cannot be excluded because of their age. The similarities are there and they must be dealt with accordingly. An additional purpose is to corroborate the linguistic evidence of the older runic inscriptions which suggests a greater age for these inscriptions, e.g. the value of the 13th rune ⇂ and the spelling *ai* for dative *o*-stems (4.3). This evidence cannot be ignored because of some foregone assumption that the runes came into being after the birth of Christ. The undeniable relationship between the runic writing system and the archaic Greek and Latin systems only serves to support, and not contradict, the linguistic evidence.

Aage Kabell was only too well aware of the pitfalls and problems of searching for the origin of the runes when he entitled his article on that subject 'Periculum runicum'. It is with his skepticism toward the ad hoc postulates of mainstream runic scholarship and convinced of the soundness of Antonsen's linguistic approach to the problem that I proceed.

7

1. SURVEY OF THEORIES ON THE ORIGIN OF THE RUNES

1.0. Introduction

The principal theories dealing with the origin of the runic alphabet are traditionally divided into three groups: the Latin, the Greek, and the North Italic, also known as the Etruscan theory. Along with these three, an additional group must be recognized, which for lack of a better all-encompassing term, I shall call 'miscellaneous'. These groups are furthermore traditionally identified by their major proponents: Wimmer and Pedersen for the Latin theory; Bugge and von Friesen for the Greek theory; and Marstrander and Hammarström for the North Italic theory. Askeberg begins to bridge the gap to the miscellaneous group, at the forefront of which stands Erik Moltke, who believes that the runes were inspired by the Latin alphabet in Denmark.

Following theories concerning the origin of the runes through the years, one seems to be confronted with a development similar to an atomic reaction which has attained critical mass. One theory produces an idea which, once hurled out, strikes into another theory. This impact gives rise to other theories which randomly collide, sometimes with the original theory itself, and cause even more theories and ideas to be generated. Aage Kabell was perhaps aware of this problem when he, in 1967, entitled his theory on the origin of the runes *periculum runicum*.

In this chapter, I will present the main theories concerning the origin of the runes from the three traditional schools of thought in chronological order and afterwards the 'miscellaneous' (1.6) group. I will outline the derivations of the runes from various alphabets in so far as the representative scholars do so. (See Table 1 which summarizes the principal derivations of the runes from various alphabets.) My intent, however, will not be to reiterate their theories in their entirety, but rather to present their theories in so far as it is necessary to gain an insight into the

9

1. Survey of Theories on the Origin of Runes

rationale behind them. Where appropriate, I will also present opinions concerning the age of the fuþark and various epigraphic features, such as direction in writing, which have been bandied about since the 19th century.

In the interest of minimizing confusion, I will reserve critical comments on these theories until after they have been presented. For the sake of historical accuracy, I will try to maintain original terminology and to clarify terms, where necessary, by the use of parentheses, e.g. muta (= stop).

1.1. The Latin theory: Ludvig Wimmer

Ludvig Wimmer first sought to derive the older fuþark from a Latin model in 1874 in *Runeskriftens oprindelse og udvikling i Norden*, which also appeared in 1887 in a revised German edition, *Die Runen-schrift*. The oldest attestations of runic writing, according to Wimmer, stem from what he called 'die ältere eisenzeit', the period from 400 to 650 A.D., which is now referred to as the older Germanic iron age (see Brøndsted 1940). Wimmer stated that the runic alphabet was modelled after the Latin alphabet no earlier than the end of the 2nd century after Christ and no later than the beginning of the 3rd century after Christ. This adoption happened in one place and was accomplished by one man of a Germanic tribe occupying southern territory near the Romans and was then spread to the other Germanic tribes (Wimmer 1887:176). Adolf Kirchhoff (1854:3) had suggested the 1st century after Christ as the time of the borrowing of the runes from Latin, but he offered no explanation for his dating.

Wimmer suggested his dating of the late 2nd/early 3rd centuries after Christ because he did not believe that with the facts available to him any inscription could be older than the 4th century after Christ. He selected the younger Latin alphabet of Imperial Rome as the prototype for the runic alphabet by default. He held Etruscan to be much older than the first runic inscriptions and therefore excluded it. Greek influence on

10

1.1. The Latin theory: Ludvig Wimmer

the Germanic peoples, in his opinion, was younger; how much he did not specify. The Greek alphabet should also not come into consideration because the Greek symbols from which runes could have been derived belonged to the Bronze Age (Wimmer gave no dates) and therefore are much too old to coincide with the first runic writings. By eliminating Etruscan and Greek, Wimmer was left with the Latin alphabet. The archeological evidence which showed Roman influence in its full strength at the end of the 2nd century and the beginning of the 3rd century after Christ led Wimmer to posit the younger Latin alphabet of 23 letters as the prototype for the runic alphabet. His derivation (1887:172) is reproduced on Table 1.

1.1.1. Wimmer's derivation. A feature led Wimmer to select the Latin alphabet of the late 2nd century/early 3rd century after Christ to the exclusion of other Mediterranean alphabets was the correspondence of the Latin letter F to the rune $\mathnormal{F}$, a suggestion made already by Kirchhoff (1854:5) and Bredsdorff (1822:7). Wimmer wrote (1887:94), 'aber nur das runenalphabet und das lateinische gebraucht dieses zeichen mit der eigentümlichen bedeutung f', i.e., that both symbols represent a voiceless labio-dental fricative. Greek and non-Latin Italic alphabets, however, had used F to represent the semivowel *w*. As a corollary to this, Wimmer (1887:94-5) stated that runic $<$ *k* corresponded to Lat. C in that they are both voiceless whereas Gk. Λ *g* represents their voiced counterpart.

I would like to draw particular attention to Wimmer's derivations for runic Q, P, $\bowtie$, X, $\diamondsuit$, K, P, S, Y, J, and M, as these derivations are exemplary of the tautological arguments used not only by Wimmer but also by other runologists.

1.1.1.1. Runic Q is derived from Lat. O. In this derivation, the runic form $*\diamondsuit = \mathsf{O}$ should be expected, but as this would lead to confusion with runic $\diamondsuit = \eta$ Wimmer (1887:107; see 1.1.1.5) assumes that legs were added to $*\diamondsuit$ to yield Q. Here, as in the case of other runes, Wimmer seems to believe in what I shall call a pre-runic form, i.e. an intermediate stage between Latin and the attested runic forms.

11

1. Survey of Theories on the Origin of Runes

1.1.1.2. Runic Þ is derived from Lat. D. Lat. D represented a muta (= stop) for which there was no directly corresponding sound in Common Germanic ('gemeingermanisch') because *d* at the time of the first inscriptions, 400 to 650 A.D. (Wimmer's dates) was supposedly a spirant. Lat. D was free to be used in representing another sound which it approximated, namely Common Gmc. þ Þ (Wimmer 1887:108).

1.1.1.3. Runic ᛗ is derived from Lat. D by means of doubling runic Þ which is ultimately derived from Lat. D. Runic ᛗ more closely represented its Latin model D in that the branches extended the full length of the staff (Wimmer 1887:109).

1.1.1.4. Runic X is derived from Lat. C. The runic form X corresponded optically most closely to Lat. X but Lat. X is too far removed phonetically to serve as a model for runic X. The Latin letter G represented a muta which did not correspond to the Common Germanic spirant and for other reasons could not be used for runic X (see 1.1.1.8). Wimmer (1887:114-5) saw in the rune X the same principle at work as with runic ᛗ, i.e. the doubling of an already adopted symbol. Runic X, he posited, is derived from the doubling of a turned runic < and subsequent joining, one atop the other at their vertices: X.

1.1.1.5. Runic ◇ is derived from Lat. C. This form occurred by doubling runic < and joining it face to face, i.e. at the obtuse ends: <>. Wimmer (1887:115) reached this conclusion on the basis of the so-called 'offene form' ⟨͟, found on the Thorsberg and Vimose chapes, in contrast to the 'geschlossene form' ◇, found on the Vadstena stone. Wimmer's 'offene form' was later established to be a form of the *j*-rune (see Friesen 1918). By interpreting this 'offene form' as a forerunner of the later 'geschlossene form', Wimmer was able to explain the lack of conclusion between the early version of ᛜ, i.e. *◇ = O which permits his derivation of runic ᛜ from Lat. O (see 1.1.1.1.). Wimmer used this rune ◇ = η to further support his belief that the runes came from Latin rather than from Greek. He explained that if the runes had stemmed from a Greek alphabet, the writers of runes would have followed the Greek practice of doubling *g* to express η as Wulfila had done when he developed his alphabet (see Marchand 1959; 1973).

1.1.1.6. Runic ᚲ (from runic * ᛗ) is derived from Lat. ᛈ .
In Wimmer's original Danish work (1874), he employed a doubling
principle which yielded runic ᚲ by combining two ᛒ 's face to face
to give ᛉ , which was supposedly reduced to a similar graph: ᚲ . In
his revised German edition (1887:117-9), however, he discarded this
theory in favor of a derivation from Lat. ᛈ , whose pocketed form
ᛈ (= | plusᴐ) was changed into a form with a staff and a crook (|
plus ᵛ). The crook was then attached to the top of the staff yielding
* ᛗ . By the time of attestation, this form * ᛗ received an additional
crook at the base of the staff to yield a fancier ᚲ , a practice which he
also saw in ᚺ ~ ᚻ and ᛉ ~ ᛋ .

1.1.1.7. Runic ᛈ is derived from Lat. Q . In his earlier
Danish version (1874), Wimmer derived runic ᛈ from Lat. ᛈ
because of an obvious optical similarity. In his 1887 edition, he altered
his thinking and categorically proclaimed Lat. Q to be the model for
runic ᛈ . Wimmer's explanation (1887:120) reads as follows:

> Dieser buchstabe [Q] wird ja in verbindung mit V mit
> dem laute ausgesprochen, der auf jeden fall auf das nächste
> dem germanischen w entsprach, und es lag daher nahe, den
> buchstaben Q selbst, der sonst in der runenschrift keine
> verwendung finden konnte, mit der bedeutung w aufzu-
> nehmen. Dass dies wirklich geschehen ist, wird in hohem
> grade durch die form der w-rune wahrscheinlich gemacht;
> sollte Q nämlich zum gebrauch für die runenschrift umge-
> bildet werden, so ist es klar, dass ᛈ so nahe wie möglich
> lag, wenn man nicht eine form wählen wollte, die mit ᛦ
> zusammenfiel.

1.1.1.8. Runic ᚴ , ᚼ is derived from Lat. G . Wimmer
(1887:126) stated that since Lat. G was not used as the basis for runic
ᚷ 'wegen der ganz verschiedenen Aussprache...müssen lat. g und
germanisches j in vielen fällen zu der zeit, als das runenalphabet gebildet

13

wurde, nahezu im laute zusammengefallen sein'. Whatever the original form of runic *j* might have been, it developed into ᚼ as seen on the Kragehul spearshaft and the Istaby stone (Wimmer 1887:121-8).

1.1.1.9. Runic Ψ is derived from Lat. Ζ . The branches of Lat. Ζ were made to start from the middle of the staff, as is the case with Lat. Ϝ to runic ᚦ (Wimmer 1887:128-34).

1.1.1.10. Runic ᚸ is derived from Lat. Υ . The rune ᚸ is achieved by taking the branches of the Latin letter and placing one at the top of the staff and the other at the bottom but on the other side. Lat. Υ (which is angular to begin with) was not borrowed directly in its original shape into runic alphabet because of the assumed principle, 'dass die nebenstriche sich niemals über den hauptstab erheben' (Wimmer 1887:136). Wimmer (1887:135) discarded theories that this rune could have stood for a diphthong *eu* because the other diphthongs were represented by their constituents: *ai* = ᚠᛁ and *au* = ᚠᚢ . He also did not believe that ᚸ could have represented *ī*, as no length distinction was made in the graphic representations of other vowels. Wimmer finally concluded that this rune was taken into the runic alphabet to preserve the symmetry of the three families and functioned, when needed, as an ideograph.

1.1.1.11. Runic ᛗ is derived from Latin ‖ (Ε). As the usual Lat. Ε would have been too difficult to reproduce in the runic alphabet, a more peculiar form of Lat. Ε was taken, namely ‖ and connected by a line, yielding ᛗ (Wimmer 1887:102).

1.1.2. Wimmer: Direction of writing. Wimmer (1887:145) prefaced his discussion on the direction of writing in the runic inscriptions by stating that 'die runeninschriften beobachten bezüglich der richtung der schrift kein festes princip'. In observing that the direction of writing in runic inscriptions runs from left to right, from right to left, as well as in snake-like boustrophedon, he added that the direction of writing in the runic inscriptions does not agree with Latin practice: 'Dies stimmt gewiss nicht mit dem lateinischen überein, wo die schrift seit den ältesten zeiten ohne ausnahme von links nach rechts geht' (but see 3.7).

1.1. The Latin Theory: Ludvig Wimmer

Wimmer assumed that the inventor of the runic alphabet wrote from left to right as did the Romans and that later on other runewriters deviated. He drew upon the example of Greek practice where the Greeks changed the original direction of the Semitic alphabet and wrote from left to right. He (1887:146) added, 'und es wird wohl kaum jemand behaupten wollen, dass es für die Griechen natürlich gewesen sei, die richtung der semitischen schrift zu verändern, aber unnatürlich für unsere vorfahren dasselbe mit der lateinischen zu thun'. The reason for inconsistency in the direction of runic writing and a lack of correspondence in this practice between runic and Latin inscriptions is purely superficial ('rein äusserliche gründe'). Wimmer reasoned, however, that despite variance in the writing direction, writing from right to left or boustrophedon is by no means a sign of great age: 'keineswegs wie bei den griechischen ein zeichen von hohem alter der inschriften' (Wimmer 1887:146; but see 2.5), but rather a sign to the contrary.

The direction left to right is standard practice in non-Nordic runic inscriptions. Wimmer cited as evidence for this statement the following inscriptions: the Bucharest ring (= Pietroassa), the Charnay clasp, the Nordendorf clasps I and II, the Osthofen, Freilaubersheim, Friedberg, and Engers clasps, as well as the old English inscriptions. He pointed out, however, that the names on the Müncheberg (= Dahmsdorf) and Kowel spearheads and the runes on the Körlin ring run right to left. To the group of inscriptions written from left to right, Wimmer counted among the oldest Nordic inscriptions the Thorsberg chape, the Strårup neckring, the Himlingøje clasp I, the Vimose comb, the Kragehul spearshaft, and the Gallehus gold horn. Wimmer, while assigning the above-mentioned inscriptions to the oldest Nordic ones, provided no dates for reference. I must assume that he assigned them to his 'ältere eisenzeit', 400 to 650 A.D.

In this group of oldest Nordic inscriptions, Wimmer included the Vimose buckle, which he read as follows (1887:147):

15

1. Survey of Theories on the Origin of Runes

l a a s a u w i ŋ a

ɐ s ɐ ᛪ ɐ ϙ ɐ ɐ

My concern here is not with Wimmer's transliteration (for a more ac-
curate transliteration, see Antonsen 1975, no. 99), but with his noteworthy interpretation of the writing direction. The direction of writing on
the Vimose buckle is of the type which Lillian Jeffery (1961:49; see 2.5)
would call false boustrophedon. Because of this boustrophedon-type,
Wimmer held that this Vimose inscription contained two separate lines,
since the runes faced foot to foot and not head to foot as in the typical
boustrophedon. Although Wimmer's work predated Jeffery's by some 80
years, he (1887:144) recognized this phenomenon when he wrote:

> Eine eigentümliche art von bustrophedon in schlangen-
> wendungen, wo die zeilen nicht bloss in entgegengesetzter
> richtung laufen, sondern wo auch die buchstaben in beiden
> reihen umgekehrt gegen einander stehen, kommt ab und zu,
> wenn auch sehr selten, in griechischen inschriften vor.

Wimmer emphasized that many of the runes, e.g. $\times$, H , $\dagger$,
I , etc., had the same form regardless of whether they were written
facing left or right. The reversibility of runes gave rise to the practice of
writing lines from right to left or from left to right. This practice of
writing lines in either direction then resulted in the use of boustrophedon:

> Der entwicklungsgang, den wir auf den denkmälern ver-
> folgen können, ist also der, *dass die ursprüngliche richtung
> der runenschrift von links nach rechts war, wie die der
> lateinischen schrift: aber früh hat man ihr daneben auch die
> richtung von rechts nach links gegeben. Durch eine
> vereinigung dieser beiden formen entstand später das
> gewöhnliche bustrophedon, und gleichzeitig damit zeigen*

16

1.1. The Latin Theory: Ludvig Wimmer

> *sich auch die ersten spuren der schlangenförmig gewun-*
> *denen schrift.*

(Wimmer 1887:159)

Boustrophedon, however, could not have developed until after rune-writers began to write from right to left, in addition to the original direction left to right (Wimmer 1887:151).

1.1.3. Wimmer: Bindrunes. Wimmer discussed the use of bindrunes as a feature already present in the oldest Nordic inscriptions. He cited the bindrune ᛗ from the Thorsberg chape and also pointed out that the two runes involved, namely ᛖ *e* and ᛗ *m*, belong to two separate words, *wajemariʀ*. The use of the bindrune here, according to Wimmer (1887:168), is to show that *wajemariʀ* represents a single concept.

The tendency to use bindrunes in general arose from their use in the word *erilaʀ*. Wimmer (1887:168) cited ᛖᚱᛁᛚᛉ from the Kragehul spearshaft, ᛖᚱᛁᛚᚨᛉ from the Varnum (= Järsberg) stone, but also ᛖᚱᛁᛚᚨᛉ from the Lindholm bone piece which shows no use of bindrunes. The abundant use of bindrunes on the Krage-hul spearshaft and the Varnum stone, Wimmer stated, was perhaps determined by their role in these presumably magical inscriptions.

1.1.4. Wimmer: Interpunction. In discussing the types of separation marks ('trennungszeichen') used in runic inscriptions, Wimmer divided these marks into two groups: (1) the more common dots, and (2) other, less common symbols.

Dots are the most common marks used and are arranged vertically in groups of one, two, three, or four, e.g. •, :, ⁝, ⁞ . Some inscriptions which contain dots are the Gallehus gold horn, the Vadstena bracteate, the Vimose woodplane, and the Charnay clasp.

According to Wimmer, the second group of less common symbols includes X on the Möjbro stone, ˀ and ✶ on the Skåäng stone, and ∧ on the Tørvika stone A.

The symbol X on the Möjbro stone is interpreted as a separ-

ation mark by Wimmer on the basis of its much shorter height in relation
to the other runes in this inscription. Wimmer also saw in the symbol
� X a relationship to the common younger runic symbol X which
was used as a separation mark in the younger runes. He (1887:166, note
1) cited the Hedeby stone as proof. The dots however, in this supposed
symbol X have not been reported by other runologists, who read this
inscription as *frawaradaz anahahaislaginaz* (see Krause 1966, no. 99;
Antonsen 1975, no. 11) with an ordinary *g*-rune, X .

The symbols ⁷ and ✶ on the Skåäng stone were seen as types
of separation marks by Wimmer. The first symbol ⁷ resembles a
superscribed Arabic numeral 7. The second symbol ✶ , which
resembles the *a*-rune of the younger fuþark, cannot be read as *a* for the
time of this inscription. Its resemblance to the younger runic ✶ is only
coincidental: 'Es besteht natürlich auch die möglichkeit, dass ✶ auf
dem steine von Skåäng nur durch einen reinen zufall dieselbe form
bekommen hat, welche die alte *jāra*-rune später annahm' (Wimmer
1887:166, note 2). This symbol must further serve as a mark to separate
hari ŋa from *leugaʀ*:

> Wir haben hier offenbar denselben namen wie auf dem
> kamm von Vimose, und durch ein zeichen, das damals kaum
> als lautzeichen im gebrauch war, sich aber doch im futhark
> befand und später zeichen für die *a*-rune wurde, hat man ge-
> wiss diesen namen deutlich von dem folgenden *leugaʀ*
> scheiden wollen, dessen ursprung ich indessen nicht sicher
> erklären kann' (Wimmer 1887:166).

The symbol Λ on the Tørvika stone A is interpreted by Wimmer
(1887:166-7) as a separation mark. It occurs above and between the
second *a* and *w* in the inscription *laðawariŋaʀ*. Wimmer (1887:167)
recognized its similarity in form to the *u*-rune but preferred to dismiss it
as a rune. 'Dass das zeichen, welches über ⊐ ⊏ steht, und eine
auffallende ähnlichkeit mit der *u*-rune hat, als eine art trennungszeichen

1.1. The Latin Theory: Ludvig Wimmer

zwischen *laða* und *wariŋaʀ* gebraucht ist, bezweifle ich nicht'.

In his remarks on the use of separation marks, Wimmer stresses throughout that he sees neither rhyme nor reason in the use of such marks. He attributed their use to the mood of the rune-writer and the latter's own personal taste. To determine the identity of any foreign model, according to Wimmer, would be very difficult. Since he held that the runes were derived from Latin, he further held that the rules regarding the use of any separation marks in the runes are those governing the use of these marks in Latin (1887:167; but see 3.10):

> aber da die runenschrift aus dem lateinischen alphabete entstanden ist, so ist es ja das natürlichste auch anzunehmen, daß die grosse abwechslung, welche die runeninschriften aufweisen, doch im grunde von dem einzelnen punkte ausgeht, der bei den Römern regel geworden war.

1.1.5. Wimmer: Rune-names and their order. Wimmer took up another point in support of his theory on the Latin origin of the runes. The order of the runes and their division into three families of eight, a practice not paralleled in the Mediterranean alphabets, as well as the names of the individual runes, e.g. ᚠ = **fehu*, ᚢ = **uruz*, etc. (see 4.8), posed a problem for Wimmer's Latin origin. To explain this apparent drastic innovation in the runic alphabet, Wimmer implied a developmental progression in the acquiring of the alphabet from the Phoenicians. The Greeks took their alphabet from the Phoenicians with the Phoenician names of the letters and the Phoenician order; the Romans took only the order of the letters from the Greeks but not the Greek names (see 3.2); lastly, the runic alphabet adopted only the forms of the Latin letters, while inventing some new graphs, e.g. ᚷ from Lat. C , but discarded the Latin order as well as the Latin names (Wimmer 1887:141). Wimmer (1887:142) attributed the deviation from the Latin model to a conscious act on the part of the inventor of the runes: 'eine mit bewustsein vorgenommene abweichung vom lateinischen alphabete'.

19

1. Survey of Theories on the Origin of Runes

He (1887:142) also suggested that the ultimate impetus for such a change was the magical use of the runes:

> Welche gründe den alten runenmeister bewogen haben, die lateinische buchstabenfolge aufzugeben und gerade die zu wählen, welche wir in dem ältesten runenalphabete finden, und ferner, warum er die 24 runen in 3 abteilungen ordnete und den runenzeichen die namen gab, die wir vorfinden, können wir jetzt natürlich nicht bis ins einzelne entscheiden. Vieles deutet jedoch darauf hin, dass die runenschrift von anfang an *nicht bloss als buchstabenschrift, sondern auch und vielleicht wesentlich zu magischem gebrauche* gedient hat.

1.2. The Greek theory: Sophus Bugge

Sophus Bugge, in his derivation of the older runic alphabet (see Table 1), saw a conglomerate of influences and traditions. He (1913:111) rejected Wimmer's theory that the runic alphabet was derived totally from the Latin alphabet of Imperial Rome: 'Men heraf har Wimmer (og flere med ham), som jeg tror, med urette draget den Slutning at Runeskriften ene og alene stammer fra den latinske Skrift'. Bugge (1913:112) believed rather that the runes are partially derived from Latin and partially from Greek, because not only do certain runes seem to derive more easily on the basis of the Greek form but also because certain Germanic sounds correspond to Greek and not to Latin. Bugge compared the views of previous scholars, who had dated the birth of the runes to the 6th century before Christ, as proposed by George Hempl (1899; 1902), with Wimmer's proposed date of 400 A.D. Bugge (1913:96) chose to side with the archeologist Sophus Müller (1897:560), who had dated the earliest Danish finds to the middle of the 4th century after Christ.

Bugge (1913:97), while recognizing the affinities of the runic alphabet with southern European alphabets, rejected the possibility of a

20

1.2. The Greek theory: Sophus Bugge

close contact in Denmark between the indigenous population of Denmark and a southern European people which, in his mind, made Denmark an unlikely place for the birth of the runes. The introduction of runes in Denmark could not have taken place later than the end of the 3rd century after Christ. The only possibility was that the Goths, who lived near southeastern Europe and would have had contact with writing peoples, after having learned to write in runes (see to the contrary Marchand 1959), transmitted this knowledge to other Germanic peoples. Bugge further believed that it was the Goths who gave the runes their names, but that it was an Armenian who taught the Goths the runes as they had been used by Galatian-speaking people in Galatia or Cappadocia. It was also this Armenian who established the order of the runes and their division into three families (Bugge 1913:185):

> Det er én Mand, en Goter, som har dannet Runenavnene efter et bestemt og gjennemført Princip. Det er ogsaa én Mand, som har bragt de 24 Tegn i en bestemt Rækkefølge, som begynder med *fuþark*. Men det er ikke godtgjort, at Rækkefølgens Opfinder er den samme Mand som Runenavnenes Opfinder eller at han er en Goter...Hvis min Forklaring af Runerækken er rigtig er det *ikke* en Germaner, som har forenet de 24, dels fra den latinske, dels fra den græske Skrift hentede Skrifttegn til ét Skriftsystem. Og det er da en Armenier, som har dannet den bestemte Rækkefølge, som begynder med fuþark.

Bugge based his hypothesis that the inventor of the runes was an Armenian on the relationship of the runic sequence *f, u, þ, a, r, k* and an Armenian word *p'ut' a-tark'* which means 'Buchstaben der Eile, d.e. kursive Bogstaver'.

1.2.1. Bugge's derivation. In maintaining that the runic alphabet was derived partially from Latin and partially from Greek, Bugge (1913:120) assigned the runes for *f, h, r,* and *j* to the Latin group, and *ŋ, g, o,* and

21

e to the Greek group, but the *w*-rune to a script more eastern than the Latin: 'Runen for *w* har jeg betegnet som overført fra en østligere Skrift end den latinske'.

1.2.1.1. Runic ᚠ is derived from Lat. F and not from Gk. *vau* Ϝ because the Greek graph Ϝ represents *w* (Bugge 1913:108).

1.2.1.2. Runic ᚺ is derived from Lat. H and not from Greek, as the Greek graph H in use in southeastern Europe at the time when the Goths lived there did not represent *h* (Bugge 1913:109).

1.2.1.3. Runic ᚱ is derived from Lat. R because the *r* which the Goths would have known, i.e. tailless P from Greek, would easily have been confused with runic ᚹ *w*. Bugge (1913:110) cited Wimmer on this point.

1.2.1.4. Runic ᛃ is derived from Lat. G in accordance with Wimmer's theory (see 1.1.1.8). In addition to Wimmer's argumentation, however, Bugge (1913:110) contended that Lat. *g* before *i* and *e* was pronounced in the same fashion as Gmc. *j*, thus making possible the use of Lat. G as the model for runic ᛃ *j* (but see 3.5). As further support for this contention that the graph for *g* can be realized by the graphs *j* or *g*, Bugge (1913:111, note 1) cited the use of the letter *g* for the sound *j* in Old High German and Old English.

1.2.1.5. Runic ᛝ is derived from the Greek practice of representing *ŋ* by writing ΓΓ *gg*. Bugge, as did Wimmer, erroneously interpreted ᛝ as a variant of ◇. In using the form ᛝ, Bugge explained the derivation from Gk. ΓΓ as a complementary juxtaposition, i.e. inset, of the two Gk. Γ 's. The need for such a rearrangement of the original Greek model arose out of a principle in runic writing that double consonants are not written: 'et Princip i Runeskriften, som sjælden fraviges, at to identiske Tegn ikke skrives ved siden af hinanden i samme Ord' (Bugge 1913:113).

1.2.1.6. Runic X is derived from Gk. X . Bugge based this assumption on the obvious visual similarity between runic X and Gk. X and ultimately on Isaac Taylor's hypothesis that at the time when the runic alphabet arose, Gmc. *g* (the result of the first shift from IE **gh* to Gmc. **g*) had not yet developed into a full stop (see Taylor 1879:36, 80). Bugge (1913:116-7) stated:

> Ligesom Runen for *g* (den tonende Spirant) efter min Mening er opstaaet af det græske Tegn for Χ , som havde beslægtet Lydværdi, saaledes skrives omvendt i frankiske og andre oldtyske Kilder *ch* ofte for etymologisk berettiget *g*.

1.2.1.7. Runic ᛟ is derived from Gk. Ω , which in the monumental form had developed legs akin to runic *o* (Bugge 1913:118).

1.2.1.8. Runic ᛗ is derived from cursive Gk. μ . Bugge (1913:119) accepted von Friesen's derivation of this rune (see 1.3.1.4).

1.2.1.9. Runic ᚹ is derived from the Georgian alphabet. Bugge's principal reasoning (1913:136) in this derivation rested upon the correspondence of the Gothic name for this rune, **winja,* to the Georgian name of the graph which represented *w,* i.e. *win.* The importance of this derivation for Bugge was that it demonstrated that the runic alphabet could not have arisen solely from Latin because the runic alphabet, like the old Greek, Phoenician, and others, had a separate letter to designate the semivowel *w*. Here, Bugge (1913:117) referred to the fact that where Latin used V for *u* and *w,* the runes had two separate graphs, namely ᚢ and ᚹ .

1.2.2. Bugge: Direction of writing. Bugge made no categorical statements on the direction of writing in the older runic inscriptions but simply made the observation that many of the older inscriptions, e.g. the Kowel spearhead, the Müncheberg (= Dahmsdorf) spearhead, the Körlin ring, the Tomstad stone, the Opedal stone, are written from right to left while others, e.g. the Vimose chape, the Kragehul spearshaft, the Øvre Stabu spearhead, the Vetteland stone, which he also counted among the oldest inscriptions, are written from left to right. Bugge, however, suggested a greater age for the direction left to right when discussing the

1. Survey of Theories on the Origin of Runes

Varnum (= Järsberg) stone.

In referring to the part of the Varnum (= Järsberg) inscription which reads *runoz waritu* and runs

Bugge called this boustrophedon writing 'denne eiendommelige Skrivemaade'. Although he voiced the opinion that this 'peculiar manner of writing' may have been due to lack of space on the stone for writing this part of the inscription in one continuous line, he (1913:23) proposed the following:

> Men man tør antage, at Anvendelsen af denne eiendom-
> melige Skrift her tillige er foranlediget ved, at Runeristeren
> kjendte en lignende Skrivemaade fra ældre Indskrifter; thi da
> Varnum-Indskriften har saa mange Overensstemmelser med
> Tune-Indskriften, saa kan heller ikke Overensstemmelsen i
> Valget af en slangeformet Dreining af Linjen være tilfældig.

In other words, the boustrophedon on the Varnum (= Järsberg) stone emulated an older practice, i.e. the boustrophedon on the older Tune in-scription, for which Bugge proposed no dating any preciser than to say that the Varnum inscription is 'noget yngre'.

The practice of writing from right to left and left to right brought Bugge to the conclusion that the persons who taught the Goths to write also imparted to them the notion that a person could write from right to left and viceversa (Bugge 1913:176):

> Det synes mig rimeligt, at Goterne af de fremmede Lære-
> mestre, som gav dem Kundskab om de Skrifttegn, efter hvil-
> ke Goterne dannede Runerne, har faaet Meddelelse om, at
> man kunde skrive baade fra høire mod venstre og fra venstre
> mod høire.

1.2. The Greek theory: Sophus Bugge

In spite of this view, however, Bugge agreed with Wimmer that boustrophedon was an innovative practice in runic writing, therefore assuming that they did not learn boustrophedon from the people who originally
taught them to write (Bugge 1913:177):

> Det eiendommelige Skifte i Skriftens Retning paa Tune-
> Stenen, som jeg med Wimmer...og v. Friesen...snarest holder
> for en Novation indenfor Runeskriften, synes at kunne
> forklares deraf, at det forud for denne Indskrifts Tilblivelse
> var (som vi tør formode) sædvanligt i samme Kreds af Rune-
> ristere og i indbyrdes nær beslægtede Indskrifter eller endog i
> Indskrifter af én og samme Runerister paa én og samme
> Gjenstand snart at skrive fra høire mod venstre og snart fra
> venstre mod høire.

1.2.3. Bugge: Bindrunes. In discussing bindrunes, Bugge made no
generalized statements about their purpose, such as that they might have
to do with magic. He stated (1913:20) that a bindrune of more than two
runes was rare in the older inscriptions, and he mentioned inscriptions
where he read bindrunes, e.g. the Thorsberg chape, the Kragehul spearshaft, the Varnum (= Järsberg) stone.

1.2.4. Bugge: Interpunction. According to Bugge (1913:24), interpunction is not used regularly in runic inscriptions. When employed,
interpunction may occur several times in a single inscription or be left
out where it might be expected. He further indicated that interpunction
served as a means for indicating word and section divisions in an inscription. Among those elements which Bugge counted as interpuncts
are spacing, dots, lines, and crosses.

   Bugge held that larger spacing between two runes indicated a word
boundary (Ordadskillelse). For example, he divided the inscription,
gutaniowihailag, from the Bucharest (= Pietrossa) ring into *gutani o*
wi hailag. He separated *wi* as a word on the basis of spacing between
the *o* and the *w* and between the *i* and the *h*. He separated *o* as a

25

word on the basis that he interpreted it as a word: 'Jeg opfatter ogsaa *o* som et eget Ord, men dette kan ikke sikkert støttes ved Mellemrummet mellem denne Rune og den foregaaende Rune *i*' (Bugge 1913:24, note 2).

Bugge (1913:24-5) pointed out without further discussion the use of dots arranged vertically in groups of one, two, three, and four on, for example, the Reistad stone, the Myklestad stone B (= Myklebostad), the Lindholm bone piece, the Vadstena bracteate, the Roes stone, the Vimose woodplane, the Osthofen fibula, the Tomstad stone, the Fyrunga stone (= Noleby), the Varnum stone (= Järsberg), and the Gallehus gold horn.

One and two vertical lines appear as division marks on the following inscriptions: the Charnay clasp, the Freilaubersheim clasp, the Kragehul knifeshaft, and the Ødemotland bone fragment (Bugge 1913: 25-6).

Cross-like marks seldom appear as division marks according to Bugge (1913:26). Among the inscriptions containing these marks, Bugge counted the Möjbro stone, the Flistad stone, and the Myklebostad stone A (= Myklebostad).

Bugge (1913:26-7) remarked that interpunction may also have functioned as an indicator of either the end of an inscription, as on the Lindholm bone piece, the Tjurkö bracteate, the Skåäng stone, and in the Veblungsnes cliff inscription, or the beginning, though this is less frequent, as on the Nydam arrow shaft, the Bezenye fibula B, Stephens' bracteates no. 52 (= Vedby), no. 31 (= Fyn 11), and no. 91 (= Geltorf bracteate 11).

1.3. The Greek theory: Otto von Friesen

Otto von Friesen, together with Bugge and initially inspired by Bugge's hypothesis that the runes were a combination of Latin and Greek characters, laid the groundwork for the Greek theory on the origin of the

1.3. The Greek theory: Otto von Friesen

runes. Von Friesen was disturbed by the fact that the oldest runic finds stemmed from northern and southeastern Europe and not from central Europe as one might expect if the runes had been transmitted from Latin or some North Italic script via the Celts. Von Friesen (1904; 1913; 1931; 1933) proposed that the runes originally and principally stem from a classical Greek cursive script in the first half of the 2nd century after Christ. He (1933:14) further supposed that this cursive Greek script had an epigraphic character attributable to its having originally been written on wax tablets with a stylus or carved in wood, plaster, clay, or metal with some sharp object. Using Salin's (1904) archeological findings, von Friesen sought the mother alphabet of the runes in southeastern Europe and set out to prove graphologically what in his mind had already been demonstrated archeologically – the runes came from a cursive Greek script.

As did Bugge, von Friesen (1913:180) believed that the Goths were the first who learned to write in runes. They accomplished this while serving in Roman legions:

> I de romerska ståndlägren ha goterna haft rika tillfällen att lära sig grekiska och latin. Grekiska och romerska vapenbröder ha varit deres läromästare, men dessa obildade soldater behärskade knappast fullständigt – när de icke voro analfabeter – någon annan skrift än det dagliga lifvets.

The runic alphabet was first and foremost designed for Gothic (Friesen 1933:38). Von Friesen based this statement on what he called the runes' inner structure ('runskriftens inre byggnad'; 1933:7), a structure which revealed itself in the graphs for *ŋg, j, w,* and two different symbols for *e,* namely М and ν .

The runes, however, did not rely solely on the Greek cursive script for their prototypes. Where Greek lacked graphs for particularly Germanic sounds, or where runes derived from Greek could be confused with other runes which had already been derived from Greek, the Latin alphabet served as a back-up source (Friesen 1933:13):

1. Survey of Theories on the Origin of Runes

> Sammanställning av de enskilda runorna med de klassiska språkens bokstäver har visat att det grekiska alfabetet ligger till grund för runorna och att det latinska alfabetet anlitats endast om det grekiska språket saknade enhetligt tecken för ljud som germanskan ägde och behövde i skrift återgiva (*h*, *u*) eller om användning av grekiskt tecken skulle vållat, att olika germanska ljud måsta betecknas med samma runa (*r*, *f*).

1.3.1. Von Friesen's derivation. My discussion will be limited to von Friesen's derivation of the runes for *ŋg, j, w,* the two *e*'s, *h, u, r,* and *f,* as these derivations form the crux of von Friesen's argument. (His complete derivation is summarized in Table 1.) The *ŋg-, j-, w-,* and the two *e*-runes prove, according to von Friesen, that the runic alphabet traces its origin to the Greek cursive script, what von Friesen (1913:13) liked to call 'life's practical script'. The *h-, u-, r-,* and *f*-runes, however, show that the Goths supplemented their new alphabet with symbols from Latin.

    1.3.1.1. Runic ◇ is derived from a symmetrization of Gk. Γ Γ. This rune usually occurs smaller than other runes, which von Friesen attributed to a probable attempt on the part of rune-writers to avoid confusion with the *d*-rune, ⋈ , which in turn can occur in a form very similar to the *ing*-rune; ▯ , only bigger 'Runan *ŋg* (äldst ▯) slutligen är en symmetrisering av grek. Γ Γ . Den har regelbundet mindre än normal höjd, sannolikt av hänsyn till *d*-runan som kan uppträd i formen ▯ (⋈) av normalhöjd' (Friesen 1931:130-31; also 1904:17).

    1.3.1.2. Runic ⟨⟩ is derived from ⟨, a cursive ligature of Gk. ει. Von Friesen sought a correspondence for Gmc. *j* in Greek because Latin used Ɩ to indicate both *i* and *j*, but the runes, unlike Latin, employed two separate graphs for *i* and *j*. Greek, however, according to von Friesen (1933:8) did not even have the sound *j* except in the diphthong αι where the offglide is represented with the graph ι. Von Friesen maintains, however, that Latin names which began with *j*

1.3. The Greek theory: Otto von Friesen

such as *Iulia* were rendered in Greek with Ⅰ , ΕⅠ , or Ζ , e.g.
'Ιουλία, Είουλία, Ζουλία. He selects the digraph ει, which in cursive
script yields the ligature ϛ and which in turn greatly resembles runic
ꗊ .

   1.3.1.3. Runic ᚹ is derived from Gk. Υ . Gmc. *w* suffered
from the same problem as Gmc. *j*. The sound *w* in Latin was spelled
with V which in Latin also indicated *u*. Greek also lacked a symbol for
w because, according to von Friesen, it occurred only in the diphthongs
ευ and αυ where Greek rendered *w* with upsilon. Greeks, when
confronted with the problem of writing a Latin name which began with
the sound *w*, rendered *w* as Ο Υ , e.g. Lat. *Vespasianus* = Gk.
Ούεσπασιανός. The Goths then took the second element of the Greek
digraph Ο Υ and remodeled it according to runic principles (runskriftens principer) to yield runic ᚹ (Friesen 1931:124). Von Friesen
sees a reminiscence of the Greek practice of spelling *w* as Gk. Ο Υ
in the Pietroassa ring inscription, where runic ᛟ ᚹ = Gk. Ο Υ
(Friesen 1913:176).

   1.3.1.4. Runic ᛇ is derived from cursive Gk. *epsilon* ✝ ,
and runic Μ is derived from cursive Gk. *eta* ᴨ . This derivation
forms a central argument for von Friesen's hypothesis that the runes
come from a cursive Greek script. Although the phonetic value of the
13th rune, ᛇ , is still debated (see 4.3), von Friesen assigns this rune
the phonetic value *ä* (= [ɛ]) and derives it from cursive Gk. *epsilon*
✝ , which is short. To the *e*-rune Μ , he assigns an original value *ē*
and derives it from cursive Gk. *eta* ᴨ , which is long (Friesen
1933:9):

> Gotiskans *e*-ljud vore sålunda med grekiskans kongruenta
> eller i varje fall åtminstone paralella. När vi så finna att
> runorna ᛇ och Μ sammanfalla med vanliga kursiva
> former av gr. ε och η, är det intet djärvt i antagandet att
> runan ᛇ urspr. fick beteckna got. öppet *e*-ljud (*ä*) och
> Μ långt slutet *e*-ljud'.

In order to circumvent the problems which arise with this derivation, e.g. runic 𐌽 appears in no decipherable inscription, and [ɛ] in Wulfilian Gothic is spelled with the digraph *aí*, von Friesen makes a series of a priori statements. He assumes that, when the lowering of Gmc. /ĕ/ to Go. [ɛ] before *h* and *r* took place in the unnamed Gothic dialect for which the runes were first designed, the Goths identified this new sound with Gk. *epsilon* ✝ and used Gk. *epsilon* to designate [ɛ] in this Gothic dialect. He assumes, furthermore, that in that unnamed Gothic dialect, Gmc. /ĕ/ had not fallen together with Gmc. /ĭ/, but that Gmc. /ĕ/ had already been lowered before /h/ and /r/. The *e*-rune M , which originally designated *ē* in von Friesen's scheme, now also represents *ě* which had not been lowered in this Gothic dialect (Friesen 1931:125):

> Anta vi att i den gotiska dialekt som var runskriftens dan-
> nares *ě* och *ĭ* ännu skiljdes åt men *ě* (och kanske också *ĭ*)
> före *h* och *r* liknade *ä*, var det närmast till hands för honom
> att låta gr. ε återge detta got. *ä* (Vulfilas *ai*) men gr. η de
> slutna *e*-ljuden *ě* (som hos Vulfila övergått till eller
> åtminstone återges med *i*) och *ē*.

The following equation might prove useful at this point:

> cursive Gk. *epsilon* ✝ = runic 𐌽 = 'Go.' *ě* before *h*
> and *r;* cursive Gk. *eta* 𐌻 = runic M = 'Go.' *ē* and *e*
> elsewhere.

In continuing with his a priori statements, von Friesen proceeds to explain how this system passed from Gothic to Proto-Nordic. PG *ē* becomes Proto-Nordic *ā*, eliminating the need for runic M as an original designator for *ē* (Friesen 1933:9). The distinction between PG *e* and *i* is maintained, thereby explaining the use of the rune M for *e* and occasionally 'i icke-huvudtonigt slutljud också med lång kvantitet' (Friesen 1931:126). Go.ε did not occur in Proto-Nordic, hence there was no need for the rune ᛇ which nevertheless remained in the runic alphabet.

1.3.1.5. Runic ᚺ is derived from Lat. H . Von Friesen reasons that *h* in Wulfila's Gothic indicated only an aspirate in all positions. Aspiration, according to von Friesen, was not at all marked in the Greek which the Goths learned to write. As a graph for *h* was necessary in runic orthography to distinguish certain words, the Latin alphabet supplied its *h*-type (Friesen 1933:11).

1.3.1.6. Runic ᚢ is derived from cursive Lat. ∩ *o*. Von Friesen selects the Latin model because Greek rendered *u* as ΟΥ which also represented *w* (see 1.3.1.3) and had already served as the prototype for runic ᚹ . Lat. V *u* was not used as the model for runic ᚢ because, according to von Friesen's runic principles, Lat. V could easily have yielded a runic ᚢ or ᚹ (Friesen 1933:10). To support this derivation further, von Friesen cites the example of Lat. *Rōma* = Go. *Rūma* where Lat. *ō*, a sound lacking in Gothic, was approximated in Gothic by *ū* (Friesen 1931:127).

1.3.1.7. Runic ᚠ is derived from cursive Lat. *F* . Von Friesen is specific about the derivation of runic ᚠ from the cursive form (1931:129): 'Tecknet för bilabialt f-ljud hämtade runskriften från latinet, och man bör lägga märke till att det är det kursiva *F* ej det epigrafiska F som runans form (ᚠ) utgår från'. Von Friesen rejected Gk. *phi,* Φ , which he maintains is phonetically closer to runic ᚠ *f,* since *phi* had served to yield runic ᚦ *þ* (Friesen 1933:12)

1.3.1.8. Runic ᚱ is derived from cursive Lat. *r* *r* as opposed to Gk. *rho* Ρ , because if Gk. Ρ had served as the model for runic *r,* confusion would have arisen between an *r* derived from Greek without a tail and runic ᚹ (Friesen 1933:13).

1.3.2. Von Friesen: Direction of writing. Like Wimmer and Bugge before him, von Friesen (1933:43) says that the direction of runic writing is right to left, left to right, and boustrophedon and that the directions right to left and left to right are already present in the oldest inscriptions.

1. Survey of Theories on the Origin of Runes

With time, however, the direction left to right becomes the predominant one.

To account for the occurrence of boustrophedon in runic inscriptions, von Friesen (1933:6-7) posits that it arose from a lack of space for writing an entire inscription in one continuous line on a piece of wood. When the rune-writer approached the end of a line, he simply rotated this piece of wood and continued to write in the direction which to him seemed left to right. The visual image of the product, however, was one of boustrophedon. As supporting evidence for this argument, he posits a subset of runes ᚠ , ᚢ , ᚦ , ᚨ , ᚱ , ᚹ , ᛒ , and ᛚ which he called vertically asymmetric runes (Friesen 1931:122-3). By this he means that, if the side from which the lines proceed off the staffs is reversed from left or right, a mirror image is obtained, e.g. ᚠ : ᚵ . He contrasts this phenomenon to a rune such as the d-rune, ᛗ , which looks the same even if it is turned from right to left. The direction in which these asymmetric runes face then determines the direction in which a line is to be read, from right to left or from left to right. An ad hoc corollary ensues whereby the change from the a-rune's Greek prototype *alpha* ᚥ , which typically faces left, to the a-rune itself ᚠ , which typically faces right, is explained (Friesen 1933:8):

> De vertikalt asymmetriska teckens viktiga funktion att ange skriftriktningen förklarar varför vid ombildningen av klassiska typer – även om vi skulle vänta motsatsen som vid ᚥ > ᚠ – bistavarna alltid anbringas till höger om huvudstaven i höger- och till vänster i vänsterlöpande skrift.

Von Friesen (1933:43) also points out that if an inscription has more than one line it is not unusual that the inscription is read from bottom to top, as he proposes is the case with the Möjbro stone. The reading of an inscription from top to bottom also occurs, and he cites the Stentoften and Noleby stones as examples of this practice.

1.3.3. Von Friesen: Bindrunes. Bindrunes, according to von Friesen (1933:43), occur frequently. For the most part, a vertical staff serves as a common staff among bindrunes. Von Friesen cites, among others, ᛗᛦ and ᚴ from the Kragehul spearshaft, ᚼ from the Kjølevik stone, and ᚼᚠ from the Stenstad stone. A diagonal staff may also serve as the common staff for bindrunes, e.g. ᚷ from the Skåne bracteate 1 and ᚷ from the Kragehul spearshaft. Their use was primarily to save space and work on an inscription.

1.3.4. Von Friesen: Interpunction. On the subject of interpunction von Friesen states that the older runic inscriptions did not use interpunction ('ordskillnadstecken') as regularly as the younger inscriptions. It does occur, however, that four vertically arranged dots serve to divide words and meaningful units or groups of words ('meningar eller ordgrupper'). As examples, he cites the Tune stone, the Gallehus gold horn, and the Fyrunga (= Noleby) stone (Friesen 1933:43).

1.4. The North Italic theory: Carl J.S. Marstrander

Marstrander, a Celticist by training, was the first to posit the so-called North Italic origin for the runes. He faulted Bugge on historical and graphological grounds, maintaining first that Bugge's date, the 3rd century after Christ, was too late, and secondly that the only runes which would correspond to a 3rd century Greek alphabet from the Black Sea area consisted of runic ᛁ , ᛏ , ᛒ , ᛗ , ᚱ , ᛥ , and possibly ᚦ *d* (Marstrander 1928:87). After accepting Haakon Shetelig's 2nd/3rd century dating for the Øvre Stabu finds, Marstrander suggested that the runes by the time of these artifacts demonstrate an inner development 'paa germansk grund'. After short consideration Marstrander rejected the Latin alphabet as the forerunner of the runic alphabet because the runes contained four symbols, ᚹ , ᚦ , ᛉ , and ᚦ , which represent phonemes non-existent in Latin (Marstrander 1928:88). His conclusion leads him to the only alphabet system left – the

North Italic. He sought to support his theory archeologically by citing a bone fragment which had been found in Maria-Saal, Carinthia, bearing what seemed to be a runic inscription ᛯ ᛋ ᚠ ᛏ ᛉ ᛗ . The Maria-Saal find was later proven to be a hoax (see Pittioni 1937).

The alphabet from which Marstrander believes the runes were derived is better referred to as Celto-Latin, as opposed to North Italic, because this term reflects the conjecture behind the theory. The peoples who originally inhabited the Alpine regions of the Italic peninsula were Etruscans, Veneti, and Rhaeti, who each had their own alphabet which historically derived from the Greek alphabet. Marstrander divides the Alpine region into a western area, populated by Etruscan and Ligurian substrata, and an eastern one, populated by Venetic and Illyric substrata. Celtic peoples moved into this area beginning in the 4th century before Christ and absorbed the indigenous cultures. When the Romans began moving into this area in the 1st century before Christ, they found a completely Celticized civilization. Latin culture, along with its alphabet, began to make its mark on this area. In the 2nd century after Christ, the Marcomanni established their kingdom bordering on the Celticized Veneto-Illyrian territory, which in the meantime had been somewhat Latinized. This for Marstrander provides the historical proximity of Germanic and writing peoples in Europe (Marstrander 1928:93-7).

It was in this cultural melting pot around the Danube in the 2nd half of the 1st century after Christ that the runes arose among the Suevi, Quadi, and Marcomanni. From here the runes spread to the Goths and the North Germanic tribes (Marstrander 1928:97).

To further support his belief in a Celto-Latin origin of the runes, Marstrander (1928:118-19) explained the runes as a West Germanic phenomenon. The linguistic evidence which he proposed in support of this supposition revolves around the use of separate graphs for /u/ and /w/ and for /i/ and /j/ and the presence of two separate graphs for /e/. The w-rune and the j-rune reflect Holtzman's law, supposedly a particularly West Germanic phenomenon (Marstrander 1928:117-18). The two e-graphs, ᛗ and ᛋ , designate respectively [ɛ] and [ē] (= $\bar{e}^2$) with the

34

1.4. The North Italic theory: Carl J.S. Marstrander

latter rune having fallen out of use and having been replaced by the former one.

Marstrander's theory of a Celto-Latin origin of the runes rests heavily on the notion that the Celtic ogam, an alphabet in which 20 letters are represented by a system of notches and lines on staffs, influenced the development of the runic alphabet. Marstrander (1928:145) contends that the division of the runes into three families and the rune-names can be traced directly to the Celtic ogam, which itself was divided into three families, *aicme,* and exhibited a similar nomenclature. The ogam, as Marstrander points out, displayed a homogeneous nomenclature in that the names of the letters centered around one semantic field ('betydningssfære'), i.e. names of plants or trees. Marstrander (1928:146) then supposes that the runes' original nomenclature exhibited the same homogeneous characteristic that the ogam did. He suggests that the runic alphabet was traditionally a 'plantefuthark' and that the original names were supplanted by the names which are otherwise attested. Marstrander (1928:148) simply cast aside attested runic nomenclature by dismissing it as illogical and childish:

> Efter den opfatning av de germanske runenavne som nu raader, viser disse en broget mangfoldighet i betydning. Her er abstrakter og konkreter, gudenavn og trænavn blandet sammen i den vildeste uorden. Efter Bugge har runenavnene følgende betydninger: fe, urokse, torn, ass (gud), ridning, byld, gave, græsgang, hagl, tvang, is, aar, barlind, dans, elg, sol, Ty, birkekvister, hest, namd, vand, Yngve, odel, dag. Intet barn kunde ha satt sammen en mere forvirret navneliste. Jeg vaager at si at i et miljø som germanernes, hvor runene fra første stund av traadte i magiens tjeneste og blev en integrerende del av deres kultus, i et slikt miljø er de aldeles utænkelige disse umotiverte sprang fra det sublime til det absurde som de historiske runenavn vidner om. Det er derfor ogsaa psykologisk uforstaaelig at runenavnene i den ældeste futhark kan ha hat de betydninger som tradisjonen tillægger dem i historisk tid.

35

1. Survey of Theories on the Origin of Runes

1.4.1. Marstrander's derivation. From the Sondrio and Lugano alphabets, Marstrander posits a composite alphabet which he contended was the model for the runes. The first line (Figure 1) shows this composite alphabet and the second line indicates attested runic forms (see also Table 1):

ᚠᛒ⟨ᛁᛁᛖᚠᚱᏀᚺᛁᛑᛗᛟ⟨ᚱᛊᛖᛏᛁ

ᚠᛒ⟨ᛗᚠ ᛊᚺᛁᛑᛗᛟ ⟨ᚱ ᛊ ᛏᛘ

Figure 1: Marstrander's derivation

The above list (Marstrander 1928:103) accounts for only sixteen of the runes in the 24-rune series. Lacking are the runes and their respective models for Þ , ᚷ , ᛈ , ᛏ , ᛄ , ᛜ , ᛦ , and ᛗ . Marstrander derives these runes from several sources and with various reasonings while referring over and over to what he (1928:116, 119) calls 'en indre utvikling paa germansk grund'. For the purpose of clarity in discussion, these runes will be considered in the following order: Þ , ᛗ , ᚷ , ᛈ , ᛏ , ᛜ , ᛦ , and ᛄ .

    1.4.1.1. Runic Þ is derived from Celto-Latin D , Ð . The basis for this assumption rests on an analysis of the Celto-Latin letter D , Ð in initial and medial positions in Celtic. He states that in initial position dentals in Celtic undergo strengthening (= fortisization) and in medial position weakening (= lenisization) which accounts for variant Celtic spellings, e.g. the name *Ðirona, Sirona,* and *Dirona*. This name can then be realized as *Þirona*. Equating Celto-Latin D , Ð to runic Þ then becomes tenable in Marstrander's mind especially when he cites Ð (= þ) on the Vimose woodplane (Marstrander 1928:104-8).

    1.4.1.2. Runic ᛗ is derived from Celto-Etruscan ᛗ . The graph ᛗ was adopted from Etruscan alphabets from Sondria and Lugano where its phonetic value remains undetermined. Marstrander,

36

however, suggests that the value of Ⱈ in Etruscan inscriptions has no bearing on its adaptation in the runic alphabet. Of import, rather, is this letter's role in Celtic inscriptions, a role which Marstrander (1928:108-11) determines to be interchangeable with Celto-Latin D , Ð . The Germanic peoples then differentiated between these two letters D , Ð and Ⱈ , which represent one phoneme in Celtic, and adapted them to suit the Germanic consonantal system. Celto-Latin D , Ð becomes runic Þ but Celto-Etruscan Ⱈ becomes runic Ⱈ (Marstrander 1928:111):

> Germanerne forefandt altsaa hos sine keltiske naboer to tegn for et og samme fonem, D (Ð) og Ⱈ – det første i det kelto-latinske, det andet i de kelto-etruskiske alfabeter – og utnyttet denne dobbelthet til at skape et grafisk skille mellem þ og ð, som artikulatorisk begge stod det keltiske fonem nær.

1.4.1.3. Runic X is derived from Celto-Latin X which in the Celto-Latin alphabets functions as a guttural spirant (Marstrander 1928:112-13).

1.4.1.4. Runic Þ is derived from Celto-Latin ⱷ , ⱷ , which according to Marstrander (1928:115) represents a voiced labial spirant in the Celto-Etruscan alphabets, /b̉/. Marstrander rejected a derivation of runic Þ *w* from Venetic Ⱶ *w* because /w/ occurs in neither Celto-Latin nor Celto-Etruscan alphabets.

1.4.1.5. Runic ᛏ is derived from either classical Lat. N or North-Etruscan ⱱ . He (1928:103) concurs with Wimmer's hypothesis that runic ᛏ is ultimately a simplification of classical Lat. N so that it would not be confused with runic H *h*.

1.4.1.6. Runic ᚲ is derived from a symmetrization of Gallo-Latin Ⱶ *p*. Marstrander (1928:103) rejects Lat. P because confusion could have arisen with runic Þ *w*. He also rejects the usual form of *p* in the North Etruscan alphabets, Ⱶ , because this would have caused confusion with runic Ⱶ *l*.

1. Survey of Theories on the Origin of Runes

1.4.1.7. Runic Ψ is derived from either Lat. Z or a North Etruscan *z*-form (Marstrander 1928:116).

1.4.1.8. Runic ᛇ is derived from Lat. E . As Marstrander interprets this rune to be /ē/ (= $\bar{e}^2$), he derives it from this Latin letter which is frequently used in the Celto-Latin alphabets along with ᛁᛁ for the letter *e*. The letter becomes runic M , while the former becomes runic ᛇ based on an internal Germanic development in the early history of the runic alphabet (Marstrander 1928:119).

1.5.1. The North Italic theory: Magnus Hammarström's derivation

Magnus Hammarström, who at first intended to write a review of Marstrander's 'Om runene och runenavnenes oprindelse' (1928), actually formulated his own theory on the origin of the runes, and together with Marstrander became the main proponent of the theory that the runes came from a North Italic alphabet. Hammarström's theory (1930) proposed that the runes could most logically be derived from the North Italic alphabets of the years 150 B.C. to O, not only because of the similarities in the letters but also because of the primitive characteristics ('en mängd ålderdomliga drag') which the runes share with the North Italic alphabets. In deriving the runes from the North Italic alphabets of the first two centuries before Christ (see Table 1 for his derivation), he believed that he could explain why one might make a case for deriving the runes from the Latin and Greek alphabets. The Greek, Latin, North Italic, and runic alphabets all shared certain similarities because they all derive either directly or indirectly from the Greek alphabet, but it was only the North Italic alphabets which maintained the primitive characteristics of the ancient Greek alphabet; and it is these primitive characteristics which prove the umbilical connection between the runic and North Italic alphabets.

Although Hammarström (1930:37-8) criticized Marstrander for relying too heavily on Celtic influence to explain the origin of the runes,

38

he did not totally exclude this possibility. He preferred to consider the runes as having been adapted from the North Italic alphabets which consisted of letters from the original Etruscan alphabets mixed with and heavily influenced by Latin letters. Two runes, ᚠ and ↑ , are clearly Latin in origin because there are no such letters in the North Italic alphabets. Other runes stem from North Italic alphabets which in turn had been influenced by Latin letters: ᚦ , ᚱ , < , ᛒ , ᛗ , and ᛩ . The majority of the runes are North Italic which, in turn, come down from the Etruscan alphabets: ᚨ , ᚠ , ᛈ , ᚺ , ᛏ , ᛁ , ᚤ , ᛋ , ᛗ , ᛕ , and ᛜ . The last group in Hammarström's derivation consists of the runes ᛋ> , ↓ , ᚴ , and ◇ , which were newly created. The *g-*, *j-*, and *η*-runes were created by suppletion ('supplerade runor'), while the 13th rune ↓ and the *p*-rune were created by differentiation ('differentierade runor'). The 13th rune, which represented a sound between /i/ and /e/, was a reformation of the *i*-rune. This reformation occurred because there was no corresponding sound in any of the North Italic alphabets (Hammarström 1930:32-3). The *p*-rune, ᚴ , was created by reforming the *b*-rune, ᛒ , i.e. by turning its pockets inside out. The runic alphabet could not assume the *p*-graph from the existing North Italic alphabets because the North Italic form, ᛣ or ᚠ , would have caused confusion with the other runes, namely the *l*-rune ᛚ and the *u*-rune ᚨ (Hammarström 1930:44-5).

1.5.2. Hammarström: Direction of writing and epigraphic practices.
Hammarström saw further evidence for his theory that the runes stem from a North Italic alphabet in the direction of writing in runic inscriptions, in the practice of not designating double consonants, and in the use of interpunction. He claimed that the only writing system which did not settle on the left-to-right direction of writing in the period during which the runes arose was the North Italic. According to Hammarström (1930:53-6) the right-to-left direction of writing among the Etruscans came ultimately from the Etruscans' teachers, the Greeks, and the North Italic system preserved this direction long after the Greeks had aban-

doned it.

As to the use of double consonants in writing, Hammarström (1930:56-7) claims that the Greeks had introduced the use of double consonants already in the 7th century before Christ, and the Romans with Ennius in the 2nd century before Christ. As in runic practice, however, the only people who did not designate double consonants in writing were the Celts.

Concerning the use of dots and strokes to indicate divisions in inscriptions, Hammarström (1930:57) remarks that such a practice was an archaism for the Greeks of classical times, while Romans used one dot to indicate divisions in texts. Among the North Italic systems, however, Hammarström finds the use of one, and three vertically arranged dots, as well as vertical strokes, to mark word divisions. The use of such dots and strokes is also found in runic inscriptions. He also noted that for the most part words in North Italic inscriptions were written together with no breaks as in the runic inscriptions.

1.6. Other theories

1.6.1. The Latin theory revisited: Holger Pedersen.

Pedersen, who actually was the first major opponent to Wimmer's, Bugge's and von Friesen's hypotheses concerning the origin of the runes, challenged all three theories. At first he concurred with Wimmer's view that graphically the runes seemed best related to the Latin alphabet while rejecting the Greek hypothesis of Bugge and von Friesen. He (1923:75) rejected Bugge's hypothesis because it proposed a Greek alphabet suppleted with Latin letters as the mother of the runic alphabet. Pedersen (1923:78) further questioned the logic of Bugge's notion of the Galatian writing teacher: 'Men når Goterne boede dör om dör med Grækerne, havde de ingen brug for Galatere til at give dem besked om bogstaverne'.

Pedersen's principal objection to von Friesen's theory lies in von Friesen's pairing of Greek graphs with their corresponding sound with graphically similar but phonetically dissimilar, runes, e.g. Gk. Χ /x/

with runic X /g/ (Pedersen 1923:70). In fact, a Greek origin of the
runes does not come into question for Pedersen, because the forms of the
Greek letters necessary for a correspondence to runic forms are too
early: 'At gå tilbage til den gamle tid, da Grækerne brugte digamma kop-
pa, og da H havde betydningen *h,* vilde være ganske urimeligt; til så
fjærne egne nåede det græske alfabets indflydelse ikke i denne gamle
tid'.

    After concurring with Wimmer's basic hypothesis, Pedersen
(1923:78) criticizes Wimmer for so quickly dismissing the possibility of
a Gallic intermediary between the Romans and the Germanic peoples in
teaching the Germanic people to write on the basis of the Latin alphabet.
Among the Latin, ogam, and runic alphabets, Pedersen sees a connection
which centers around the name for the graphic designation of *b.* He
maintains that the Greek nomenclature for letters, *alpha, beta,* etc., was
the basis for determining letter names in western European scripts.
Hence, Gk. *beta* sounded like the Gallic word for birch which in Celtic
began with *bet-. The Celtic word was then translated by the Germanic
peoples and became the name of the *b*-rune, ON *bjarkan* (Pedersen
1923:78-9). Pedersen (1923:43-4) draws four analogies between the
runic and the ogam alphabets: (1) their division into families; (2) both
alphabets deviate drastically in the sequence of the letters; (3) both
alphabets have a graph for *ŋg;* and (4) both alphabets have full names
('lange bogstavnavne') for the individual letters.

    From these analogies and similarities which both the runic and the
ogam alphabets share with the Latin, Pedersen (1923:79-80) concludes
that both the Irish and Germanic peoples developed their alphabets in
Gallic schools somewhere on the Rhine around the beginning of our era
under the direct influence of the Latin alphabet:

> Og jeg vil da i tilslutning hertil opkaste det spörgsmål om
> ikke nogle av de mange analogier mellem runer og ogam
> kunde have en dybere grund deri, at såvel Germanerne som
> Irerne havde lært at læse hos Gallerne. At nogle av analo-
> gierne er rent tilfældige, er på forhånd klart. Således

41

overensstemmelsen i tegnet for *ŋg*. Men den leg med bogstaverne, som ytrer sig i inddelingen av alfabetet i avdelinger
med fuldstændig ophævelse av den latinske bogstavfølge,
kunde det ikke have været en idræt, som øvedes i Galliens
skoler?

1.6.2. The Latin theory displaced: Fritz Askeberg. As a reaction to
the theories of the Latin, Greek, and North Italic origin of the runes,
Fritz Askeberg (1944) posited an hypothesis which on the one hand
rejected the major theories, but on the other, proved to be another variant
of the Latin theory. His hypothesis states that the runes were developed
by the Goths in the 2nd century after Christ when they lived on the
Vistula and that the Goths modeled the runes after the Latin alphabet
(Askeberg 1944:85). He believed that the methodology of his
predecessors was at fault in that they all sought a one-to-one
correspondence between the runes and the mother alphabet: 'Futharken
är ej en slavisk kopia utan röjer sig genom de enskilda tecknens
utformning och gruppering, som en tämligen fri omarbetning av
förebilden' (Askeberg 1944:78).

Askeberg divided the runes into three groups ᚠ , ᚢ , ᚱ ,
ᚲ , and ᚺ , which must come from Latin; ᚦ , ᚨ , ᛈ , ᚷ ,
ᛏ , ᛁ , ᛋ , ᛊ , ᛉ , ᛒ , ᛗ , ᛖ , ᛚ , ᛋ , and
ᛜ , which can come from Latin; lastly ᚲ , ◇ , and ᛟ , which
were newly created (Askeberg 1944:83). Askeberg (1944:79) admits that
the differences between the runes and the Latin, Greek, and North Italic
alphabets were striking ('påfallende'), but he maintained that these differences cannot be accounted for by assuming that the runes underwent a
long development prior to the first runic attestations, as von Friesen
suggested. In fact, Askeberg (1944:63, 77) totally rejects a long period
of development for the runes on the basis of their primitive characteristics. He characterizes the period of the oldest finds as 'en typisk öv-
nings- och förberedelsestid' because of the isolated and often meaning-
less letter sequences which represent the oldest runic attestations and in-

fers that the oldest runic finds represent the runes as they were first invented.

The answer then to the runes' origin must be sought by examining the geographical and archeological backgrounds ('geografiskt och kulturellt fristående miljö'; Askeberg 1944:79). In his 1944 work, *Norden och kontinenten i gammal tid,* Askeberg rejected earlier theories while railing against German scholarship for considering central Europe as the runes' birthplace. He rejected these theories because (1) there were no early runic finds in central Europe and (2) there were no early runic finds in the Black Sea region. Without early runic finds to support an hypothesis for the runes' origin, the hypothesis, in Askeberg's opinion, must be rejected.

The oldest runic finds which he records come from Øvre Stabu in Oppland (Norway), Mos on Gotland (Sweden), Dahmsdorf in Brandenburg (Germany), Kowel in Volhynia (USSR), and Rozwadow (Poland). Geographically, these finds point to the Vistula region and northwards (Askeberg 1944:80). Archeologically, he disputes Salin's dating of fibulae with a retroflex foot ('tillbakaböjd fot') to the time after the Goths' departure for southern Russia and accepts Bolin's and Forssander's dating which places these fibulae prior to the Goths' departure to the Black Sea (1944:81). The location of the oldest finds together with archeological evidence leads Askeberg to his conclusion that the Goths developed the runes in the 2nd century after Christ.

1.6.3. The Danes did it: Erik Moltke. Erik Moltke, who expounded on Askeberg's original hypothesis, first posed the question, 'Er runeskriften opstået i Danmark?' in 1951. At first, he put forth his question in a speculative light and wondered if the runes might not have ben invented by a Dane. He suggested that the runes represent an independent development partially inspired by the Latin alphabet (Moltke 1951:52-3). He seemed more frustrated than enlightened by runic scholarship prior to his own. He (1951:53) stated that 'det har også altid stået for mig som en gåde, at man ikke har villet tillægge runernes opfinder så megen intelligens, at han var i stand til selv at komponere tegn som ᛏ , ᚲ ,

1. Survey of Theories on the Origin of Runes

↓ og X i et alfabet, der kun må operere med lodrette og skrå streger'. He employed Askeberg's reasoning and said that if we take the Vimose finds, the oldest runic finds, which are dated to the end of the 2nd century after Christ, and assume a 200-year period during which there are no finds, we are at the beginning of an era in Danish history, referred to as the Roman Iron Age, when Roman culture began to make its mark on Denmark (Moltke 1951:54).

In 1976 and 1985, Moltke restated his speculations with greater conviction and summarized them in eight points:

1. The presence of two designations for *i*, | = *i* and ↓ = *ī* < *ei*, show that the runes could not have been invented later than the end of the 2nd century after Christ.

2. Because the oldest known inscriptions, according to Moltke, come from ca. 200 A.D., we must assume that the runes came into existence approximately 200 years earlier. With an additional grace period of 100 years, the birthdate of the runes is placed in the period from 100 B.C. to 100 A.D. (He later changed this dating after the discovery of the Meldorf fibula to 0 + 50/-100; see Moltke 1981; 1985:64-5.)

3. Chronology excludes any possibility of the runes coming from the Phoenicians. Principles of writing also exclude the Greek and Etruscan theories.

4. The alphabet which served as the model for this inventor of the runes was the Latin capitals of Imperial Rome. Some of the runes are direct copies of Latin capitals, while others are imitations and a third group consists of newly created letters (Figure 2).

Identity in both form and sound:
Latin: B F H I L R T V – runes: ᛒ ᚠ ᚻ ᛁ ᚱ ᚱ ↑ ᚾ

Similarity in both form and sound:
Latin: A C (or K) D M O S – runes: ᚠ < ᚦ ᛗ ᛉ ᛊ

Similarity of form but not of sound:
Latin: P M X – runes: ᚹ = *w*, ᛖ = *e*, ᚷ = *g*.

1.6. Other theories

Runic forms unknown in Latin:

ᛏ = *n*, ᛡ = *j*, ᛀ = *ï*, ◇ = *ng*, ᛈ = *p*, ᛉ = *z*, ᛗ = *d*.

Figure 2: Moltke's derivation (1985:59)

5. The runes do not show the same order of letters as do other alphabets.

6. The runes have the same primitive characteristics as other alphabets in their primitive stages: irregularity in height of letters, no set direction in writing, and irregularly used interpunction.

7. Points 4-6 show that the fuþark could not have originated in the proximity of classical alphabets.

8. Denmark is the logical place for the birth of the runes because a large number of the oldest finds are from there. The runes may be considered as an independent development whose impetus stems from the Rhine region. The basis for their development was the Latin capitals of Imperial Rome (Moltke 1976:54-5).

1.6.4. The Greek theory reevaluated: Isaac Taylor and George Hempl.
George Hempl, who was one of Wimmer's earliest critics on this side of the Atlantic, was also one of the earliest proponents of the view that the runes stem from the Greek alphabet. He regretted that Taylor's earlier work on deriving the runes from a Thracian alphabet of the 6th century before Christ (Taylor 1879) had been ignored by the scholarly world and attempted to revive it with some modification.

Taylor believed that the runes were borrowed from the Greek alphabet before or during the first part of the Germanic sound shift (Grimm's Law) and based this belief on his comparison of the runes with their alleged pre-shift phonetic values with Greek letters, e.g. runic $<$ *k* from IE *$*g$* equals Gk. *gamma* $<$. Hempl then modified this theory so that the runes reflect a stage in Germanic wherein the Germanic obstruent system had not yet completely undergone the second part of the shift (Verner's Law; see Hempl 1902). This chronology then enables Hempl to account for discrepant correspondences between the runes and Greek letters, such as runic ᛞ *d* equals Gk. ⊗ *theta* and runic ᚦ equals Gk. ▷ *delta.*

Hempl, however, first sought to explain the connection between the runic and Greek alphabets by literally juggling with the order of the runes. He claimed that the runes had been ordered in the fuþark on a principle of associating like forms with like forms and like sounds with like sounds. For example, runic ᚠ *f* had usurped the original position of runic ᚨ *a* in the alphabet because the two runes looked alike and thus became confused. Runic ᚢ *u* became the second rune in the fuþark because Gmc. *b* was a bilabial fricative more similar to *w* which is close to the vowel *u*. Runic ᚦ *th,* which derives from Gk. ▷ *delta,* occupies the third position in the fuþark. The order which begins to emerge is *a, b, d,* etc., i.e. *alpha, beta, delta,* etc. (Hempl 1899:371-2).

Hempl also accused Wimmer of not allowing the 'archaic features of the runes their due weight' (Hempl 1899:373) and maintained that these features, e.g. direction of writing, must be dealt with. Hempl's reasoning then led him to the conclusion that the runes were borrowed from a western Greek alphabet in the 6th century before Christ.

1.6.5. Periculum runicum: Aage Kabell. Aage Kabell, whose theory Klaus Düwel (1983:91) termed 'phantastisch!', later took up Taylor's and Hempl's view that the runes came from a Greek alphabet of the 6th century before Christ (Kabell 1967:116). Kabell also tried grappling with the problem of the rune sequence within the fuþark and proposed that the runes were originally arranged according to 'graphische Attraktion' (Kabell 1967:105). This graphic attraction caused certain runes which had common features originally to be grouped with each other. Kabell (1967:108, 111) posited an 'Urschrift' in which the first family was arranged according to hook and staff: ᚢ , ᚦ , ᛃ , ᚹ , and ᚲ ; the second, double staves: ᚺ and ᛋ ; and the third, double hooks: ᛏ , ᛒ , ᛗ , ᛗ , ᛖ , ᛜ , ᛟ , and ᛞ . The runes not accounted for in his 'Urschrift' came into existence by means of derivation. The graph ᚼ , either *s* or *i* in Greek, depending on the Greek alphabet in question, served as the basis for runic ᛏ , ᛁ , ᛉ , ᛋ , and ᛊ (Kabell 1967:109-10). The entire system of grouping and differentiation arose out of a pedagogical device (Kabell 1967:114):

> So hat ein Schriftgelehrter dann einmal die Elemente der griechischen Buchstaben mit Vermeidung gekrümmter und horizontaler Striche seinen vor- und frühgermanischen Freunden gegenüber gruppiert, die Gefahren der möglichen Verwechselungen hervorgehoben und die notwendigen Differenzierungen durchexerziert.

1.7. Summary and remarks

Throughout the preceding pages, I have dealt with a summary of research concerning the origin of the runes. Although there have been attempts to explain the origin of the runes prior to Wimmer (see Worm 1651; Benzelius; 1724; Bredsdorff 1822; Kirchhoff 1854), Wimmer formed the basis from which later theories have arisen. These theories either took a stance in favor of him, with modifications (see Pedersen 1923), or against him. Wimmer grappled with the problem of deriving the runes neatly from Roman capitals of the 2nd and 3rd centuries after Christ. By restricting himself to this time period, he forced himself into the position of dealing with alphabets from that time period. Based solely on his time reference, his theory must immediately fall into disrepute because, in 1972, a runic inscription was discovered on the Meldorf fibula, which has been dated archeologically to the 1st quarter of the 1st century after Christ (Düwel 1981; Düwel/Gebühr 1981), Bugge's and von Friesen's theories, which respectively set the runes' birthdate to the end of the 3rd century and the 1st half of the 2nd century after Christ, must also be discounted.

Wimmer's, Bugge's, and von Friesen's theories must furthermore

1. Survey of Theories on the Origin of Runes

be held suspect, each, however, for varying reasons. The mental gymnastics which each goes through in order to yield forms from a parent alphabet to the runic alphabet is, to say the least, awkward and confusing. Of the Latin, Greek, and North Italic theories, Wimmer's is the only one which consistently dealt with one alphabet. Bugge, von Friesen, Marstrander, and Hammarström supposed a mixture of alphabets. They take one letter from alphabet a, another from alphabet b, and perhaps another from alphabet c. This methodology of selecting letters from various alphabets was principally used in the North Italic theories by Marstrander and Hammarström, but by no means is this practice restricted to them. Consider Bugge, who derived some runes from Latin, some from Greek and one from Asia Minor. Of such a practice, Moltke expressed his opinion quite amply during the taped discussion which followed papers presented at the First International Symposium on Runes and Runic Inscriptions (Thompson 1981:16):

> Regarding the mention of the Mediterranean alphabets, Moltke dismissed the Etruscan theory as 'stupid', pointing out that... in order to create the runes from Etruscan letters the inventor would have had to wander from one Alpine tribe to another, borrowing one rune here and another one there.

Von Friesen not only derived the runes, a clearly epigraphic script, from the Greek and Latin alphabets, but also from both monumental and cursive scripts within these alphabets.

Many runologists discussed here have suggested that an intermediary who was neither Germanic nor a native speaker of the language whose alphabet was being taught played a role in teaching some Germanic person to write. Bugge's suggestion of a Greek-speaking Armenian intermediary enabled him to account for the order of the runes on the basis of a word in Armenian while still deriving the runes from Greek. Marstrander suggested Celtic peoples because the later, more or less uniformly attested names of the runes make no sense – to him. Because of the division of runes into families, as in the ogam – and the

1.7. Summary and remarks

meaning of *ogam* and *rune* is supposedly the same, namely 'secret' —
the original runes must have had names translated from Celtic. These
names were since then replaced by the uniformly attested names. He
does not consider the fact that the ogam does not employ letters per se as
do the Greek, Latin, and North Italic alphabets. The ogam system is
similar to the cryptic runes found on the Rök stone. Marstrander's actual
derivation of the runes, however, does not proceed from the ogam itself
to the runes, but rather from the Latinized Celto-Veneto-Illyrian alphabets of northern Italy.

Hammarström, criticizing Marstrander for placing such importance
on the role of the ogam, simply discarded that aspect of Marstrander's
theory. Hammarström, however, did maintain the validity of Marstrander's basic assumption, but his reasoning differed. He cited the
primitive characteristics of the runic inscriptions as proof that the runes
derive from the North Italic alphabets. Here again, Hammarström's
dating for the birth of the runes confined him to the period from 150 to
0, during which only the North Italic scripts wrote from right to left, did
not designate double consonants, and used division marks most similar
to those used in runic inscriptions.

Hammarström, as did Wimmer, Bugge, von Friesen, Marstrander,
Pedersen, Askeberg, and Moltke, saw Lat. ᖴ as the only possible
source for runic ᚠ *f* because only Latin used this letter to indicate /f/.
These runologists were all aware of Gk. *digamma* ᖴ , a bilabial, but
readily dismissed it because of its great age. To derive runic ᚠ from
Gk. ᖴ would place the birth of the runes several centuries into the
period before Christ. A reluctance to assign the date of the birth of the
runes to a period much earlier than the birth of Christ seems to permeate
runic scholarship. Erik Moltke originally set the date for the runes' birth
at the year 0 ± 100 but immediately qualified this statement: 'Sandsynligheden taler imidlertid ikke for, at man skal på den anden side af år
0' (Moltke 1976:54). With the discovery of the Meldorf fibula, he was
forced to revise his dating to 0 + 50/-100 but again qualified his statement (Moltke 1981:7):

1. Survey of Theories on the Origin of Runes

It is common practice to place the birth of the futhark about two hundred years earlier than the oldest inscription found; this is undoubtedly a reasonable contention, a sort of safety valve. But no one can deny that there is a possibility that an inscription from the very first day of the construction of the runic alphabet may be preserved and found. I think that the Meldorf fibula represents the earliest, the oldest layer of our runic inscriptions, and that the inscription on it will be the nearest we will ever come to the origins of the runes.

Moltke's dating of the Meldorf fibula is curious, because archeologists say the 1st quarter of the 1st century, and not the first half of the 1st century after Christ. Klaus Düwel also chose to expand the period which archeologists set, from the 1st quarter to the 1st half of the 1st century after Christ. Even though he admits to this dating, Düwel (1981a:13) seems ill-disposed towards accepting such an early dating:

> On the one hand, a single inscription [Meldorf] cannot bear the burden of the question of the origin of the runes. On the other hand, we know that the runic inscriptions from about A.D. 200 presuppose the development of a complete runic system of graphemes and phonemes, which can hardly be in existence before the time of the Meldorf fibula. And again: what about the gap in the discoveries between Meldorf and Øvre Stabu?

Of course, the Illerup ådal finds shed a new light on the entire matter. A desire to date the origin of the runes as late as possible may not be founded on serious, objective investigation, but rather on politics and national pride. Antonsen (1980) has already demonstrated the effects of politics and national pride in the case of transliterating the 15th rune, Y . The earliest dating suggested for the runes' birth are 600 B.C., made by Isaac Taylor, an Englishman, and George Hempl, an American,

50

1.7. Summary and remarks

and the dating 250-150 B.C. by Ralph Elliot (1959:11), another Englishman. These dates represent time periods in which it would be nigh impossible to identify any one Germanic tribe. An inability to attribute any one Germanic tribe with the development of the runes would make it equally impossible for any one national group to lay claim to the runes as their ethnic heritage.

From the 19th century to World War II, runologists developed pet theories and adhered to them. If one favored the North Italic theory, a date later than the year 0 would become tenuous because the Latin alphabet had completely taken over in the Alpine regions. If one favored a Latin or Greek theory, problems arose in accounting for the w- and j-runes because neither Latin nor Greek had symbols for these phones and Latin had no phone [þ]. Not being able to find corresponding graphs for corresponding phonemes led investigators to make ad hoc assumptions about the creation of certain runes. For example, Wimmer derived ⟨⟩ j from Lat. G , which in Latin supposedly became palatalized in certain environments. Von Friesen derived ⟨⟩ from a cursive Greek ligature ϛ εɩ because evidence from monumental Greek shows that Latin names which began with /j/ were written Ε Ι ! Deriving the runes from either a North Italic or a Latin source meant crediting a South Germanic tribe, the present-day Germans, with the development of the fuþark. Deriving the runes from a Greek source meant attributing the Goths, who supposedly came from Gotland, with the development of the fuþark.

In the period just prior to and during World War II, Germans, like Krause and Arntz, favored the North Italic theory and developed the notion of 'vorrunische Begriffszeichen'. In 1944, Askeberg, a Scandinavian, not only posited his theory which removed the birthplace of the runes from South Germanic territory, i.e. central Europe, but also lambasted German scholarship for treating the area that Tacitus called Germania as exclusively German (Askeberg 1944:88):

> Den tyska vetenskapen om germanernas etnologi och forn-
> historia har sedan länge haft en tung belastning, nämligen de

51

1. Survey of Theories on the Origin of Runes

klassiska auktorernas oändligt omdiskuterade notiser om ger-
manerna. Tacitus' Germania kommer man väl aldrig att helt
kunna frigöra sig från, så länge den håller vid liv den upp-
fattningen, att Tyskland är Germanien och den axel, kring
vilken germanernas hela historia och kultur rör sig ända från
tiden omkr. Kr. föd.

Moltke, a Dane, put forth his theory in 1951 and proclaimed Denmark
the birthplace of the runes. He said that if his notion that the runes had
been developed in Denmark were correct, then the Danes were responsible for the two great achievements in Scandinavian writing, the creation of the older and younger fuþarks (Moltke 1951:56):

Vi har nu kun at vente på fremtidige fund for at se, om Danmark atter skal træde i baggrunden til fordel for kontinentet,
eller om det kan holde sig i diskussionens brændpunkt, indtil
en til vished grænsende sandsynlighed opnås. Bliver dette
tilfældet da har Danmark fostret to store stifindere på skriftens område, den nordgermaner, der engang ca. 100 e. Chr.
skabte runeskriften, og dernæst den dansker der engang
omkr. 800 bragte en ende på den forvirring, som efterhånden
havde skæmmet den gamle 24-tegns futhark, og konstruerede
den for stenmestrene ideelle 16-tegns futhark.

A methodological problem with the theories presented in the preceding
pages arises in that ad hoc rules have been established by runologists in
order to make their theories work. For example, Wimmer, in order to derive the 13th rune ᛉ from Lat. Y invokes a principle, 'dass die nebenstriche [sich] niemals über den hauptstab erheben' (1.1.1.10). By
assuming this principle, he was able to force his derivation of this rune.
Bugge assumed that since *g* underwent palatalization before *i* and *e* in
both Latin and Old English, he could easily posit Lat. G *g* as the
model for runic ᚼ *j* and simultaneously maintain that the runes came
from Greek.

52

1.7. Summary and remarks

Hammarström was the first to use the term differentiation and suppletion to explain the occurrence of certain runes. He, however, was by no means the first to employ this method, e.g. Wimmer's derivation of the *p*-rune (1.1.1.6), von Friesen's derivation of the 13th rune ᛏ (1.3.1.4), and Marstrander's derivation of ᚦ (1.4.1.1.) and ᛗ (1.4.1.2). Moltke carried the notion of suppletion and derivation to an extreme in maintaining that some runes were freely created.

The notion of primitive characteristics became popular with Hammarström, who used it to facilitate his derivation of the runes from the North Italic alphabets. He correctly pointed out that these primitive characteristics also existed in the older Greek alphabets but rejected the Greek alphabet as the runes' source, because these characteristics in Greek had been done away with by the 4th century before Christ. It is from these primitive characteristics in Greek that I shall proceed, for they (to paraphrase Hempl) have not been allowed their due weight. An examination of the older Latin and Greek alphabets will show a striking similarity not only in the forms of the letters but also in the so-called primitive characteristics.

1. Survey of Theories on the Origin of Runes

Table 1: Summary of the derivations of runes from various Mediterranean alphabets (Friesen 1931: Table 1)

2. GREEK EPIGRAPHY

2.0. Introduction

We have seen in the preceding chapter that runologists have by and large restricted themselves to the classical alphabets of the Mediterranean when dealing with the question of the runes' origin. The Greek and Latin alphabets from the age of the Roman Empire do, however, reflect several centuries of development – a fact seldom mentioned in runic scholarship – and have undergone standardization. Except for those scholars who ascribed to one of the versions of the North Italic origin of the runes, there is little or no mention of the multiplicity and diversity in Greek epichoric alphabets. Only Hammarström hints at such a possibility in the Greek tradition, but quickly dismissed Gk. Γ *w* and H *h* as being even remotely connected with the runes because of the early period during which these letters were used in those phonetic values. If one, however, proceeds further back in time, as the discovery of the Meldorf fibula forces us to, one is confronted with a situation in the Greek tradition similar to that of the runes: no standardized alphabet (as we in the 20th century understand it), no set direction in writing, various interpuncts, the use of ligatures, and aspects of an epigraphic tradition which bear a striking resemblance to that of the runic tradition.

In the course of chapter 2, all dates refer to the time before Christ unless otherwise specified. The term archaic will refer to the period before 400 B.C.

2.1. The Greek alphabet: Background

The classical Greek alphabet, which many runic scholars seem to have in mind when discussing the origin of the runes, stems from a writing reform which took place in Athens in 403-402 B.C. under the reign of

Eucleides. He persudaded the Athenians to adopt the Ionic alphabet of Miletos as the standard alphabet. This Ionic alphabet became the classical Attic alphabet and took the following form (Figure 3).

Α Β ΓΔΕΙΗⴲΙΚΛΜ ΝΣΟΓ ΡϚΤΥΦΧΥΩ

Α Β Γ Δ Ε Ζ Η Θ Ι Κ Λ Μ Ν Ξ Ο Π Ρ Σ Τ Υ Φ Χ Ψ Ω

Figure 3: The classical Greek alphabet after the Milesian writing reform, 403-402 B.C. (Guarducci 1967:1.86)

Prior to this, and even after this reform, however, the Greek alphabet demonstrated an epichoric character, which with its multiple forms is confusing to the 19th- and 20th- century mind accustomed to standardization. Table 2 from Lillian Jeffery (1961) provides an overview of epichoric alphabets, as well as interpuncts, as they differ from one region to the next in the archaic period. Such tables, however, can be misleading in that they allow the reader to believe that these letters represent the Greek alphabet with all of its variants. For example, dotted theta ⊙ is not represented in Jeffery's table although she records it as it occurs in each local alphabet in the course of her text. Margherita Guarducci, who records dotted theta in her composite tables of Greek alphabets (Guarducci 1967:1. Tables 1 and 2), points out that dotted theta ⊙ occurs frequently already in the 6th century before Christ (Guarducci 1967:1.94). Guarducci also records theta in the form ⊖ or ⦸ in the archaic period. Another form which Jeffery records in her text and not on her table is ⊕ from a Sikyon inscription of the 5th century before Christ. She states that this form came into fashion because it was easier to cut into stone or bronze (Jeffery 1961: 138).

The differences, sometimes minuscule, in each epichoric alphabet are important for runic studies in that they show a degree of variance among Greek alphabets which has been neglected in runic studies (see Antonsen 1982). A reason for such variety was suggested by Cook and

2.1. The Greek alphabet: Background

Woodhead (1959), who attributed the lack of a standardized form to the events surrounding the inception of the Greek alphabet. They attribute the diversity in epichoric Greek alphabets to the personal nature of the alphabet itself. When the Greeks invented their alphabet, it was designed for personal use among Greek traders at Phoenician trading posts and only later did it develop into a communal phenomenon.

Opinion on the age and birthplace of the Greek alphabet differ. Rhys Carpenter (1933) represents one end of the spectrum with his dating of 720-700 B.C., while Dörpfeld (according to Guarducci 1967: 1.70) represents the other extreme with his dating of the 15th century before Christ. Guarducci herself (1967:1.70-73) favors a date between the two extremes, that is, in the 9th century before Christ because the oldest inscription, the cup of Nestroy, comes from the period 740-725 B.C. Since the materials on which the Greeks first wrote were probably perishable, she believes that one must allow at least a one-hundred year leeway in dating.

Not only does the dating of the Greek alphabet itself present a problem for the classical epigraphists, but the dating of a single inscription can often be tenuous.

A. Woodhead sets up five criteria which he feels should be considered when attempting to ascertain the date of an inscription: the provenience of the inscription, the character of the monument, the content of the inscription, formulas used in the inscription, and the forms of the letters. His fifth point is particularly pertinent for runic studies because he warns against dating an inscription on the basis of a letter form (see 4.2.0). Woodhead (1981:62) says, 'Such statements as "the lettering indicates a date towards the end of the second century B.C." or "first century A.D., on the letter forms" are familiar in epigraphic publications. But this criterion, so often used as a first resort, is much better left as a final refuge; its evidence is far less precise and secure than is popularly supposed'. He (1981:65) further states that new letter forms do not oust old forms totally, even if the new ones are very much in vogue.

In conjunction with Woodhead's statements, I refer the reader to table 2 where it can be seen that many of the boxes contain two forms of

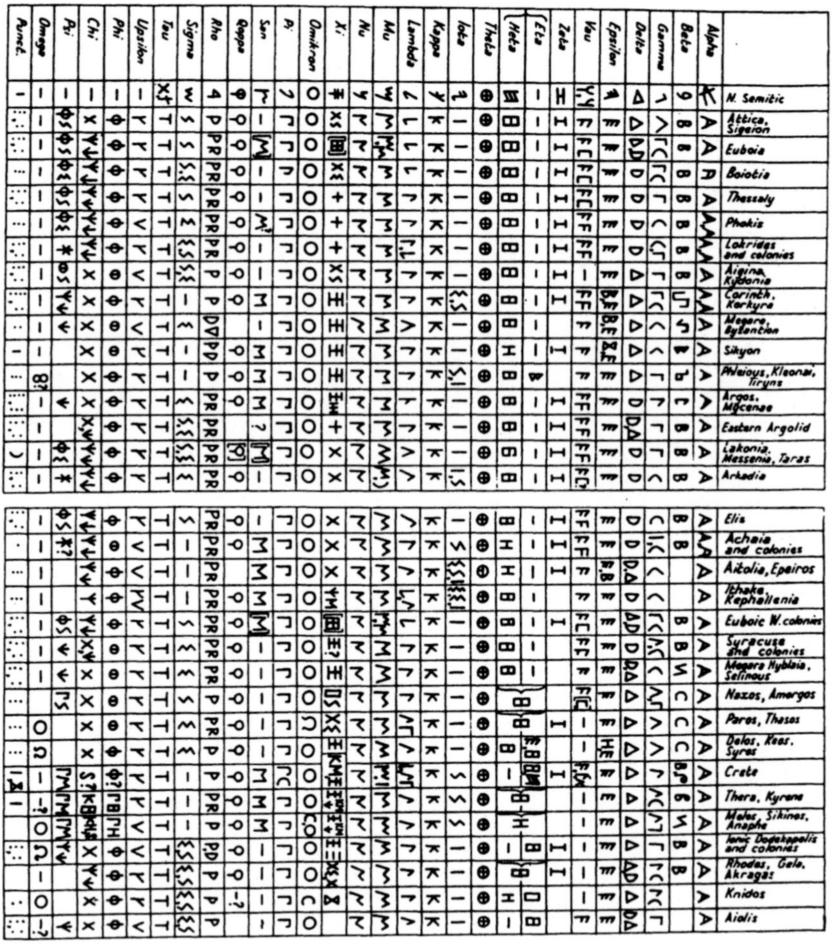

Alpha
Beta
Gamma
Delta
Epsilon
Vau
Zeta
Eta
Heta
Theta
Iota
Kappa
Lambda
Mu
Nu
Xi
Omikron
Pi
San
Qoppa
Rho
Sigma
Tau
Upsilon
Phi
Chi
Psi
Omega
Punct.
N. Semitic
Attica, Sigeion
Euboia
Boiotia
Thessaly
Phokis
Lokrides and colonies
Aigina, Kydonia
Corinth, Korkyra
Megara, Byzantion
Sikyon
Phleious, Kleonai, Tiryns
Argos, Mycenae
Eastern Argolid
Lakonia, Messenia, Taras
Arkadia
Elis
Achaia and colonies
Aitolia, Epeiros
Ithaka, Kephallenia
Euboic W. colonies
Syracuse and colonies
Megara Hyblaia, Selinous
Naxos, Amorgos
Paros, Thasos
Delos, Keos, Syros
Crete
Thera, Kyrene
Melos, Sikinos, Anaphe
Ionic Dodekapolis and colonies
Rhodes, Gela, Akragas
Knidos
Aiolis

Table 2: Archaic Greek letter forms (Jeffery 1961:Table 1)

the same letter. Jeffery indicates in her original table that a comma between two forms signifies that the first of the two is generally older. No comma indicates that the two forms coexist in this particular region. A specific example is that of *rho,* where the tailed *rho* R seems just as common as the tailless P . This point has seldom, if at all, been brought out in discussions on the connection between the runic and Greek alphabets. In fact, the tailless *rho* is often cited as evidence by runologists to dispel any connection between the runes and the Greek alphabet as proof that the runes must derive from Latin. Moltke (1985:58) seems totally unaware of it in his treatment of Greek *rho.*

2.2. Greek abecedaria from the archaic period

The following abecedaria represent the Greek alphabet in its earlier stages, from the 7th to the 5th centuries before Christ. Unlike the classical Greek alphabet, they contain graphs which were eliminated in the Milesian reform as letters but maintained in the Greek numeral system. These graphs are *vau* Ϝ , which as a letter had represented the semivowel /w/ and later as a numeral the value six (Jeffery 1961:25; Guarducci 1967:1.91-2), and *qoppa* Ϙ , which as a letter had occurred only before /o/ and /u/ and represented [k] (Jeffery 1961:33-4; Guarducci 1967:1.98). As a numeral, *qoppa* was retained in the Milesian alphabetic numeral system in the value 90. Both of these letters dropped out of use in Greek during the 5th century before Christ, but lived on in the Latin alphabet as Ϝ and Q (Guarducci 1967:1.91-2, 98).

Guarducci discusses four abecedaria which I have reproduced below: the writing tablet from Marsiliana d'Albegna (2.2.1), a cup from Samos (2.2.2), a stamnos from Metapontion (2.2.3), and a cup from Boiotia (2.2.4).

2.2.1. The writing tablet from Marsiliana d'Albegna (Figure 4), the oldest of the four, does not come from Greece, but from Italy. It was originally found in an Etruscan tomb in Etruria, but undoubtedly stems

59

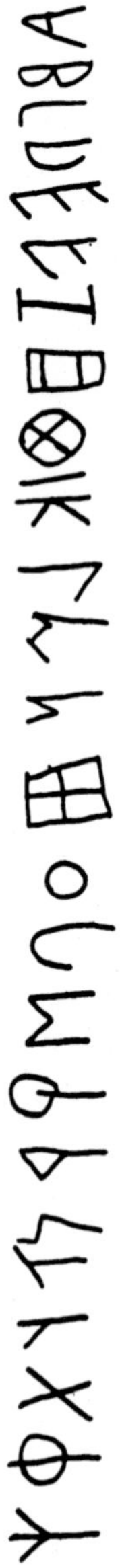

Figure 4: Abecedarium from writing tablet of Marsiliana d'Albegna (Italy), 600-500 B.C. (Guarducci 1967:1.228)

(R-L) A B Γ Δ E Ϝ Z H Θ I K Λ M N Ξ O Π M Ϙ P Σ T Y Ξ Φ X

2.2. Greek abecedaria from the archaic period

from Cuma, a Greek colony near Naples. The alphabet is carved on the border of an ivory writing tablet and is believed to have served as a model for scribes using this tablet. The tablet itself is datable to the 1st half of the 7th century. This alphabet contains 26 letters, all written in a retrograde direction with the exception of *sigma,* which unlike its classical form Σ , has only two crooks S . Jeffery (1961:236-7) indicates that in contrast to other 7th-century abecedaria in the western Greek colonies, the Marsiliana abecedarium is the only one in which the direction of writing proceeds from right to left. It is noteworthy that Guarducci (1967:1.228) holds this alphabet-type from Cuma to be the prototype for both the Latin and Etruscan alphabets.

2.2.2. The Samian cup (Figure 5) is a fragment found in a temple dedicated to Hera in Samos and is dated to 660 B.C. The alphabet is executed in a retrograde fashion around the cup. The importance of this find, according to Guarducci (1967:1.266), is the use of the letter *digamma* F in its value as a letter and not as a numeral as was heretofore believed for this region. The alphabet seems to have been written hastily and its use on the vase is strictly ornamental.

2.2.3. The Metapontine stamnos (Figure 6) is made of clay. The alphabet, whose complete circumvention of the vase is interrupted by the handles, was carved into the vase before firing. The purpose of the alphabet seems to be purely decorative. The vase itself is dated to the beginning of the 5th century. The direction of writing is from left to right (Jeffery 1961:256, no. 19; Guarducci 1967:1.116).

2.2.4. The Boiotian cup (Figure 7) from the Attic region of Greece stems from the 2nd half of the 5th century. As with the Metapontine stamnos, this alphabet was incised before firing. The alphabet is written in two lines on one face of the vase, both lines proceeding from left to right. Notable here is that *rho* has a tail (Jeffery 1961:94, no. 20; Guarducci 1967:1.446).

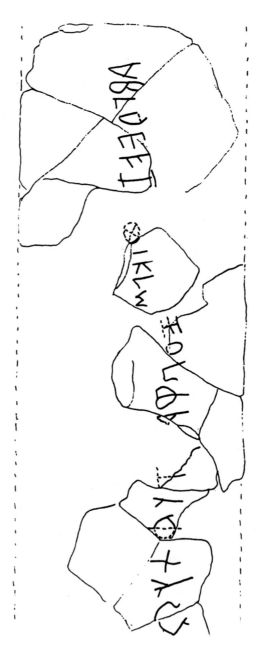

Figure 5: Abecedarium from Samian cup sherd, 660 B.C. (Guarducci 1967:1.265)

(R-L) A B Γ Δ E Ϝ Z Θ I K Λ M Ξ O Π Ϙ P T Y Φ X Ψ Ω

2.2. Greek abecedaria from the archaic period

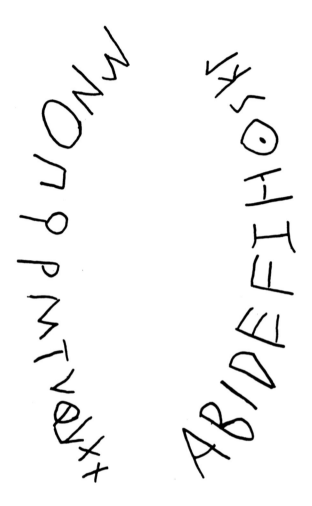

Figure 6: Abecedarium from Metapontine stamnos, ca. 500 B.C.
(Guarducci 1967:1.116)

Line 1: A B Γ Δ E Ϝ Z H Θ I K Λ
Line 2: M N O Π Ϙ P Ϻ T Y Φ X Ξ Ψ

Figure 7: Abecedarium from Boiotian cup, 450-400 B.C. (Guarducci 1967:1.446).

Line 1: A B Γ Δ E Ϝ Z H Θ I K Λ

Line 2: M N O Π P Σ T Y Ξ Φ X

2.3. The letters of the Greek alphabet and their values

Table 3 presents the archaic Greek alphabets and the corresponding phonological values for principally Attic Greek in the 8th and 4th centuries before Christ. As mentioned previously (2.2.), certain letters such as *vau (digamma)* Ϝ and *qoppa* Ϙ were lost between the archaic and the Hellenistic period. As Jeffery (1976:24) states, 'The full Greek alphabet had 27 letters. No city used the lot; they picked and chose, depending on their dialect, on the chances of transmission, and doubtless on other factors unknown to us'. Graphs such as Ϻ *san* and Σ *sigma*, which both represented /s/, seemed redundant for the Greeks. The reason for having two graphs representing the same phonemes, however, can be traced back to the Phoenician alphabet, which differentiated these graphs. Both graphs were nevertheless retained in the Greek alphabet. Jeffery (1961:1-5) offers an extremely plausible explanation for this phenomenon. She believes that humans are creatures of habit and when an illiterate learns to write from a literate person, the illiterate does not question the literate person's system of recording sound sequences. The illiterate merely imitates as best he can the literate person's graphs and sound values. He does not make changes until he has mastered the system. The learner did not quibble; he was not a philologist!

The letter forms represented in table 3 show my own stylized form. Other variants are depicted in table 2 (see also Larfeld 1914: Schrifttafel). As the Greek sound system – in as much as one can speak of a uniform system – changed from the 8th to the 4th centuries, so did the value of the letters. The phonological values, as well as the phonological-graphic correspondences, differ from dialect to dialect. For example, western Greek dialects, e.g. Boiotian, retained the letter Η in its value /h/, while Ionic (the standard alphabet) Η came to stand for /e/ because of the loss of initial /h/ in this dialect (see below). The details of such dialect differences, however, will not be discussed here since the purpose of the ensuing discussion is to provide to the runologist, unfamiliar with Greek, a brief overview of Greek letter-sound correspondences so that he may have a reference point. More detailed discussions on Greek

Table 3: Greek (Attic) letter/sound correspondences

Letter		Sound value 8th century	Sound value 4th century
alpha	A	ắ	a [a]
beta	B	b	ƀ
gamma	Γ	g	g̱
delta	Δ	d	ð
epsilon	Ɛ	ĕ	e
vau (digamma)	Ϝ	w	---
zeta	I	zd	z
heta	H	h	ē (Ionic)
theta	⊗	th	þ, th
iota	I	ĭ	ī
kappa	K	k [c]	k [c ~ k]
lambda	Γ	l	l
mu	M	m	m
nu	Ν	n	n
šin (xi)	Ξ	khs	ks
omicron	O	o	o [o]
pi	Γ	p	p
san	M	z, s	---
qoppa	ϙ	k [k]	---
rho	R	r	r
sigma	Ϛ	s	s
tau	T	t	t
upsilon	Y	u	y (Doric u)
phi	Φ	ph	ph
chi	X	kh	kh
psi	Ψ	p(h)s	ps
omega	Ω	o	o [ɔ]

66

2.3. The letters of the Greek alphabet and their values

phonology may be found in Sturtevant (1940), Brandenstein (1954), and Bartoněk (1966).

The vowels are designated by the letters A , $\digamma$, I , O , Y , and Ω . While there was a long/short distinction in Greek, the tense/lax opposition seems to have played the greater role. *Alpha* A represented /ā/. By the 4th century, however, historical /ā/. under certain conditions comes to be represented by both *alpha* and *(h)eta* because of the conditioned change of /ā/ to /e/ (Sturtevant 1940: 30). *Epsilon* $\digamma$ designated /ě/ in the 8th century. With the loss of initial /h/ in Ionian (western Greek dialects retained initial /h/), the letter *heta* H came to stand for at tense *e* [e] and $\digamma$ took over the function of representing lax *'e* [ɛ] (Sturtevant 1940:32-5; Guarducci 1967:1.91-3). *Iota* I represented /ĭ/. (Sturtevant 1940:31). *Upsilon* Y represented Gk. /ŭ/ but as /u/ underwent fronting in non-Doric, its value came to be /y/ (Sturtevant 1940:41-4). As Gk. /ou/ shifted to /u/ the digraph OY was used to represent /u/. *Omicron* O designated *o* [o], and *omega* Ω , a modified form of O , represented *o* [ɔ] (Sturtevant 1940:44).

The 8th-century voiced stops /b, d, g/ became voiced spirants / ƀ,ð, g̶/ by the 4th century and were written as B , Γ , Δ , (Sturtevant 1940:86). The voiceless stops /p, t, k/ were represented throughout as Γ , T , K , φ (Sturtevant 1940:85). Although Gk. [c] was originally designated with *kappa* K and Gk. [k] with *qoppa* φ (see Larfeld 1907:1.364-5; Guarducci 1967:1.98), the graph φ as a letter fell into disuse since the difference [c ~ k] was not phonemic (Brandenstein 1954:31).

Although the origin, development, and articulation of the Greek voiceless aspirates /ph, th, kh/ are debated (see Schwyzer 1939), they occurred as single graphs φ , $\otimes$, X , and also as digraphs, ΓH , $\otimes H$, and KH (φH) (Schwyzer 1939:2.144). This latter practice seemed to be the predominant tradition in the epichoric scripts of the Aegean Islands, especially Melos and Thera (Jeffery 1961:320; see also Table 2). Sturtevant (1940:78) cites the following forms from Thera: ΠH for φ , Πhειδιπίδας; KH for X , Ἀρκhαγέτας; and

2. Greek Epigraphy

ΘΗ   for ⊖ , as well as ⴹΗ for Χ , θαρύμα ⴹ hος.
Zeta Ι regularly represents /z/ and *san* Μ, or *sigma* Ϟ (Ϟ),
regularly represents /s/.
   Lambda Γ regularly represents /l/; *rho* Ρ (Ρ), /r/; *m u*
Μ , /m/; and *nu* Ν, /n/.

2.4. *Orthographic treatment of nasals*

The one feature which the three Greek nasals, *m, n, η*, all share is, according to Schwyzer (1939 1:1.213), 'die oft auftretende ungenaue Bezeichnung oder auch Unterdrückung der Bezeichnung in der Schrift vor
Verschlußlaut'. Although the nondesignation of nasals before stops is not
regular, its occurrence is not infrequent. Schwyzer related it to a reduced
or weakened pronunciation of the nasal before stops and cited the following inscriptional forms: Att. 'Ολυ(μ)πιόδωρος, 'Αταλά(ν)τη, νύ(μ)φη
'Ε(γ)κέλαδος, μεγάλη(ν)τε; Ion. Πό(μ)πις, Νυ(μ)φέων, Νίκα(ν)δρος; Epid.
'Ατλα(ν)τίδας (see also Brugmann 1900:76). Schwyzer also related this
orthographic practice to a tendency for the nasal to assimilate to following consonants. In all cases, however, the nondesignation of the nasal
did not indicate a loss of the nasal because the tendency was to reintro-
duce the nasal in the orthography of the standard language (Schwyzer
1939 1:1.213-15).
   While Brugmann (1900:76), and later Schwyzer (1939), included
the Cypriot and Pamphylian practice of not writing nasals before other
consonants, these practices can have little bearing on the runes, contrary
to Makaev (1965:58-9; see also 4.4.1). The Cypriots employed a sylla-
bary which had only open syllables (see Brandenstein 1954:45). Consequently, the designation of a nasal would require the addition of another
syllable, which would still not end in a nasal but rather in a vowel. A
nasal could therefore never occur directly before another consonant in
this writing system. Pamphylian is a peripheral, creolized Greek dialect
of Asia Minor and has little to do with any developments in Greek
proper (see Thumb/Scherer 1959:176-9).

2.5. Direction of writing

The designation of the velar nasal in Greek could be accomplished in two ways. The archaic spelling of η with *nu* resulted from the fact that *n* before another consonant would assimilate to that consonant's point of articulation: *n* before *g* is η. The later, more familiar, classical spellling of the velar nasal with *gamma* must have arisen where *g* occured before a nasal and became nasalized, e.g. the so-called *agma*, *gm* becomes ηm(Schwyzer 1939:1.214-15; on *agma*, see Richardson 1941). Thus Gk. *gamma* stood for η in the combinations γγ, γκ, γχ, γξ.

2.5. Direction of writing

The direction of writing in Greek can be divided into three patterns: continuous retrograde, continuous progressive, and boustrophedon. Continuous retrograde is defined as writing in which each line proceeds from right to left; in continuous progressive writing, each line proceeds from left to right; and in boustrophedon, each line proceeds in the direction opposite to that of the preceding line. The order in which I have mentioned these three categories does not reflect any chronological order.

Generally, it has been assumed that retrograde writing precedes the boustrophedon, which in turn gives way to progressive. This assumption has been based on the fact that the Semitic peoples from whom the Greeks learned to write wrote in continuous retrograde. Jeffery (1961: 43), however, asks:

> is there in fact any evidence to suggest that the Greeks origi-
> nally adopted the Semitic practice of writing continuously
> from right to left, before they evolved the method of writing
> *boustrophedon*? This is the assumption stated or implied by
> standard treatises on Greek epigraphy... It cannot be too
> strongly emphasized that the earliest surviving Greek in-
> scriptions give no warrant for this assumption of an initial
> stage of continuous retrograde script, followed after a time
> by the adoption of the boustrophedon system.

2. Greek Epigraphy

In the earliest examples of Greek retrograde, Jeffery knows of only one example of true continuous retrograde. This is a graffito from Pithekoussai, 700 B.C. (Jeffery 1961:236, no. 1).

Jeffery challenges previous scholarship which states that the oldest inscriptions run in continuous retrograde. Religious and secular codes found on temple walls in Gortyn (Crete), 600-525 B.C., seem to be continuous retrograde mixed with boustrophedon, but according to Jeffery (1961:44) are all actually boustrophedon. The apparent mixture of writing directions can be attributed to a practice on Crete of paragraphing, whereby each new clause is begun on a fresh line. If two or three consecutive clauses are no longer than one line, the visual effect is continuous retrograde. Clauses, as she points out, which are longer than one line are boustrophedon. The underlying pattern for the entire inscription, though, is boustrophedon. Although Jeffery dates this inscription to the 6th century, Guarducci (1967:1.410) suggests a dating in the 4th century.

Archaic examples of boustrophedon are to be found in the following inscriptions: a rock graffito from Thera, end of the 8th century (Jeffery 1961:318, no. 1 a); an Attic graffito from the Acropolis, 8th century (Jeffery 1961:69, no. 2); a bronze statuette from Boiotia, 700-675 B.C. (Jeffery 1961:90, no. 1); and a statue from Naxos, 650 B.C. (Jeffery 1961:291, no. 2).

Because it seems strange to the 20th-century eye, boustrophedon elicits the question: Why write from right to left and then left to right? The principal reason for the development of the boustrophedon system, as both Jeffery and Guarducci point out, is the symmetrical nature of the letters. Guarducci (1967:1.411) states:

> Uno di codesti elementi fu senza dubbio il carattere graficamente simmetrico di varie lettere del primitivo alfabeto greco
>
> (Δ I Η ⊗ I O M Ϙ T)

2.5. Direction of writing

...Tutte queste lettere si presentavano uguali sia verso destra sia verso sinistra, e favorivano perciò l'andamento della scrittura vuoi nell'un senso vuoi nell'altro.

Jeffery (1961:49-50) distinguishes between true and false boustrophedon. True boustrophedon requires that each line of an inscription face in the opposite direction to the preceding one, e.g.

This manner of boustrophedon, however, is not always present in the case of two lines proceeding in apparently opposite directions, as there are instances where, according to Jeffery, people have claimed reversal of letters when they are actually dealing with what she calls 'false boustrophedon'. False boustrophedon is found when a line appears to be written from right to left, but is in actuality written from left to right. The writer has merely turned the writing surface in a hairpin fashion and continued writing:

This is a technical simplification of the boustrophedon, because the person writing does not need to reverse the direction of the letters, for he is still writing in the same direction. (For an example of false boustrophedon, see Lakonia stele, 500 B.C., in Jeffery 1961:193, no. 31.)

Most of the boustrophedon inscriptions come from the 6th and 5th centuries but the practice is by no means limited to this period as, according to Guarducci (1967:1.409), they continue to be found even into the 4th century. Jeffery (1961:49-51) has demonstrated that boustrophedon occurs among the earlier inscription along with retrograde, which indicate that one did not necessarily predate the other. As with the Gortyn Codex discussed above, there is more often than not a reason why writing directions may appear mixed. As Jeffery (1976) later suggested, the ancients did what they did presumably because of a variety of factors unknown to us.

The practice of progressive writing became common during the 6th century and was established by the middle of the 5th century. Guarducci (1967:1.412) cites Herodotus as her source, who between 449 and 444 B.C. stated that the Greeks wrote from left to right. This practice, however, is also attested at the end of the 8th century on an oinochoe from Ithaca (see Jeffery 1961:230, no. 1; Guarducci 1967:1.274, no. 1).

Ernst Zinn (1950), however, interpreted the development in the direction of writing among the Greeks in a somewhat different manner. He believes, as does Jeffery, that in the beginning, the Greeks wrote either from right to left or from left to right. Most inscriptions at this early stage were very short, perhaps containing only a name, and did not require more than one line. As inscriptions started to become longer, people would try to squeeze the last few letters in at the end of a line as in the following example (Figure 8):

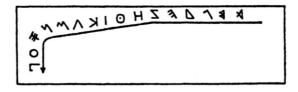

Figure 8: Writing direction (Zinn 1950:11-12)

The motivating force here was the gravity of the hand and eye. From this point, if an inscription were longer, the writer would continue writing around the edge of the writing surface, using the exterior rim of the surface as his guideline, as in the following examples (Figure 9):

2.5. Direction of writing

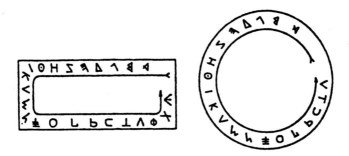

Figure 9: Writing direction (Zinn 1950:11-12)

The next progression would be to continue writing around the exterior edge and when the writer ran out of room, he would start spiraling the inscription, as in the following examples (Figure 10):

Figure 10: Writing direction (Zinn 1950:13-14)

The last step, however, could take another course. If the writing face were long and thin, the writer could swing the next line around instead of following the exterior edge of the writing surface. Zinn called this 'Schlangenschrift'. The letters of each line would face each other foot to foot or head to head much as in Jeffery's 'false boustrophedon'. The writer then continued his inscription for several lines in this 'capovolto' manner as in the following example (Figure 11):

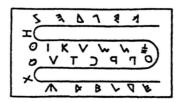

Figure 11: Writing direction (Zinn 1950:13-14)

73

2. Greek Epigraphy

From this stage, the true boustrophedon follows. Each line alternates the direction of the previous line. If the first line begins right to left, the second line begins left to right and so on, as in the following example (Figure 12):

Figure 12: Writing direction (Zinn 1950:32-3)

Once people begin writing boustrophedon, it becomes easy to settle on one set direction, either the lines are written from left to right or from right to left. The Greeks happened to have agreed upon the left to right system. The stoichedon manner of writing is in Zinn's mind the perfection of this system which is motivated by the gravity of the hand and the eye. The letters are arranged perfectly so that they are aligned horizontally as well as vertically.

2.6. Ligatures

Although the use of ligatures in Greek inscriptions from the pre-Imperial period was apparently not as great as in Roman times, their existence attests to their use and the ability of people to read them. Their more frequent use in the Roman period is owing to the influence of Rome and her own epigraphic practices which favored the greater use of ligatures (Larfeld 1907:1.408; Guarducci 1967:1.402-5).

Larfeld (1907:1.408) records the oldest use of a ligature in a 6th century inscription from Amorgos Η⌐ Γ Ο = Η Γ Γ Ο = ΙΠΠΟ, as well as in a 5th-century inscription from Naucratis (Egypt) ΡΑ̅ΟΡΕ̲ = ΗΡΑΓΟΡΕ̲ = Ηραγορε. Guarducci (1967:1.403-4), in addition, records a 5th-century Attic inscription Æ =

2.7. Interpunction

Δ E   as well as a 3rd century Delphic decree   Ρ̄ Ṃ   =
A P Ṃ A   (For examples of ligatures from the Imperial Age, see
Larfeld 1907:2.513; Guarducci 1967:1.404-5.)

2.7. Interpunction

Interpunction, defined as the use of marks to indicate word divisions in
an epigraphic text, is not standardized in Greek inscriptions. Interpunction did occur in pre-Greek epigraphic practices. The Minoan culture of
Linear B on Crete regularly employed dividing marks between words.
Semitic practice also reveals this feature, but not with the regularity of
Linear B (Guarducci 1967:1.390). The Greeks employed interpuncts
with similar irregularity. The use of dividing marks in Greek inscriptions
predominates in archaic times and confines itself principally to Attica in
Hellenic times. Interpunction disappears around the middle of the 5th
century owing, as Guarducci (1967:1.390) believes, to the flowering of
stoichedon writing. The practice then comes to life again in the Greece
of Roman times, as Klaffenbach (1957:48) points out, because of the
influence of Roman practice: 'erst das Vorbild der römischen Inschriften
bringt die Interpunktion wieder in gelegentliche Aufnahme'.

The types of interpunction can be divided into three groups: dots,
lines, and semicircles. Each type may have several variants: dots are
arranged in geometric configurations $\vdots$, $\therefore$, $\because$, $\vdots$; a semicircle
)which serves as the basic shape for interpunction in Roman times; a
line or a series of lines arranged vertically, horizontally, or obliquely | ,
− , ≷ , ≷ , ⅄ ; or a combination of dots and lines |: .

At times the dots may be superficial indentations on the writing
surface or they may be executed in such a way as to add to the ornamen-
tation of the inscription. With the increasing rarity of interpuncts, spaces
between words replace former interpuncts, but it cannot be stressed
enough that there is no set, standardized practice. As Guarducci (1967:
1.397) says: 'Infine non sarà inutile osservare che ogni regola formulata
su questo argomento resta necessariamente un po' fluida, perché la scelta

75

e l'uso dei signi divisori dipendono in larga misura dal gusto personale, e talvolta anche dalla fantasia dell'antico artefice'. (For further interpunct variants see: Larfeld 1907:1.431; Jeffery 1961, Part 3, 'Notes on letter forms' which precede each chapter).

2.8. Preparation and layout of the text

The instruments used in executing an inscription on stone depend upon the desired quality of the finished text. The most common instruments employed are the hammer and chisel. Other instruments include a dressing chisel, a borer, a compass, a square, and a rule.

Giancarlo Susini (1973) indicates that a stone writing surface would be polished before being written upon in Hellenistic and later times. The text would then be sketched out onto the writing surface and executed at first with a chisel and hammer and then refined with the dressing chisel. The other instruments would then be used as needed. Guarducci holds that the craftsman who sketched out the letters and the one who subsequently executed them was for the most part the same person. Susini, however, sees the sketching out of the text and its execution as two different crafts performed by separate people. At times the craftsman who did the actual incising of the letters would forget to chisel in letters which had been sketched on the *titulus,* i.e. the actual space reserved for writing. An example of such an omission is a Naxian statue from Delos, ca. 660 B.C. (see Jeffery 1961:291, no. 2; Guarducci 1967:1.154, note 1).

The omission of letters may be the result of a practice whereby the craftsman who executed the letters did not execute them in the order in which they had been sketched out. Instead he may have preferred to execute all letters which require the use of a compass, e.g. Θ, before proceeding to others. In this manner he could possibly skip a letter.

Once the letters have been executed, they can be colored in, usually with red or blue, at the discretion of the craftsman. Sometimes only certain letters are colored in because the craftsman wishes to high-

2.8. Preparation and layout of the text

light them. In special cases an inscription may be inlaid with gold, as in the case of Pindar's ode to Diagoras of Rhodes (see Guarducci 1967: 1.458).

Before incising the letters on a surface, guidelines would be drawn in and at times even chiseled out along with the letters as part of the finished text. These guidelines are at first horizontal, but with the flowering of the stoichedon, vertical lines are also introduced into the text.

In the case of errors, the craftsman may choose to obliterate that part of the inscription which is incorrect and reexecute it. He may write over the same area or make an addendum to the original text. The process of obliterating a text was also employed if a stone were to be reused. Such is the case with an inscription from Polyrhenia (Crete), first dedicated to 'Areus, son of Akrotatos', but whose name was obliterated for that of 'Caesar Augustus, son of the divine' (see Guarducci 1967: 1.445). If an error in a text were minor, the craftsman simply added the corrections in by color. Occasional inscriptions with such correction are preserved and show traces of the correction by color over, above, and between the lines or at the end of the text.

Günter Klaffenbach (1957:46-7) believes that the preparation and execution of a text was a meticulous process which involved revisions after the text was laid out on stone but before it was actually chiseled into the stone. In this manner, drastic corrections after chiseling could be avoided:

> Diese [Korrekturen] bestanden in Einmeißeln vergessener Buchstaben bzw. Worte zwischen bzw., über die Linie oder der radikalen Maßnahme der Rasur. Jedenfalls beweisen uns diese Korrekturen, die alles andere als selten sind, daß die fertige Inschrift in der Regel einer Revision unterzogen wurde, sei es durch den Steinschreiber selbst oder einen anderen, der für die ordnungsmäßige Durchführung der Aufzeichnung verantwortlich gemacht war.

77

2. Greek Epigraphy

2.9. Epigraphic materials

The materials used for epigraphic writing in the Greek world vary greatly. Among these materials are stone, bronze, lead, silver, gold, clay, wood, ivory, and glass. The most common preserved material by far though is stone.

When speaking of stone as an epigraphic material, a distinction must be made between bare rock and finished stone. Rocks bearing epigraphic texts occur in isolated environments near or in caves and meadows. Since these rock inscriptions contain simple religious texts, Guarducci connects them with the strong chtonic elements of the Greek religion. Rock inscriptions are also found in public places with names or simple sayings. These Guarducci (1967:1.428) believes to be the products of vanity or idleness, of someone merely wishing to write his name. At times, inscriptions of this type provide a mixture of the sacred and the profane, and even display quite vulgar tastes, such as the rock inscriptions found near the temple of Apollo Carneus and the nearby gymnasium in Thera.

The practice of writing on rocks is already attested in the 8th century and continues well into Roman times. On finished stone, which not only includes single stone items, such as stelae, cippi, columns, and statues, but also stone used in building structures, we may find laws and decrees, such as the Gortyn Codex (Crete) from the 7th century. The largest part of the stone inscriptions, however, occur on single stone objects, a practice which begins in the 7th century and, as with rock inscriptions, continues into Roman times.

Wood was also one of the most abundantly used epigraphic materials and was employed for everyday purposes, such as keeping records. In addition, wood was also made into a tablet shape with projecting borders into the center of which wax could be poured. The wax surface could then easily be reused by smoothing it out. These tablets were used for everyday purposes, e.g. letters, notes, accounts (Guarducci 1967:1.439-40). Due to the highly perishable nature of the material, most inscriptions executed on wood have not come down to modern times.

2.10. Types of inscriptions

Among the lesser used materials are bronze, ivory, gold, and silver. Inscriptions on these materials do not abound because of their prohibitive costs and luxurious nature. (For further examples and more detailed information on epigraphic materials, see Jeffery 1961:51-8; Guarducci 1967:1.429-43.)

2.10. Types of inscriptions

The contents of an inscription vary according to the intended use of the inscription or of the object inscribed. Various categories may be set up (Klaffenbach 1957:53-89; Woodhead 1981:35-51) to make the study of extant texts more manageable. Although delimiting such categories often leads to gray areas, my concern is to discuss the major classes of inscriptions which epigraphists have etablished in order to provide a general sketch of what the ancient Greeks wrote about and in what form. The categories to be discussed are: dedications (2.10.1), honorary inscriptions (2.10.2), funerary inscriptions (2.10.3), and miscellaneous (2.10.4). Epigraphists of Greek also talk about other categories, e.g. manumissions (the freeing of slaves), and public decrees. Such categories, however, are extraneous to runic studies and I shall not discuss them. For actual examples of such texts, the reader is referred to Woodhead (1981:48-51).

2.10.1. Dedications. As the heading suggests, this group of inscriptions deals with dedications. The inscribed text usually states that some person dedicates something to someone for some reason. The dedicator is expressed in the nominative case: the object dedicated, in the accusative; the dedicatee, in the dative. The dedicatee may also be expressed in the genitive case which, as Woodhead believes, indicates that the object has become the property of the deicatee. Of the nominative, dative, accusative, and verb components, all save the dative may be omitted.

Dedicatory inscriptions, as a rule, do contain a reference to the dedicator which Woodhead (1981:41) interprets to be a 'form of justifiable self-advertisement'. In very early periods, the object which is dedicated may speak for itself. Woodhead (1981:41) points out that 'there are many permutations and combinations of phraseology which ocur in this type of inscription'. A reason for the making of the dedication may be stated or simply implied. The texts may be written in prose or verse form. The verse form, however, seems to be favored in the early period.

Woodhead (1981:42) explains further that dedicatory inscriptions frequently depart from the normal continuous text. The text may be arranged in a symmetrical fashion to give importance to the name of the dedicator or the dedicatee.

2.10.2. Honorary inscriptions. To this group belong those inscriptions which serve to honor a person or deity. Woodhead (1981:42) acknowledges the thin line between what constitutes an inscription of honor and a dedication. Klaffenbach (1957:62) stated that the two groups were similar: 'denn es unterliegt keinem Zweifel, daß sich die Ehreninschriften...aus den Weihinschriften entwickelt haben'. The phraseology of honorific inscriptions take the following form. The person being honored appears in the accusative while the bestowing party appears in the nominative case. The verb may be expressed but is more often than not omitted. If a deity is involved, or later in Roman times an emperor, their names will appear in the dative case. As with dedication, the reason for the bestowal of honor may be included in the inscription.

2.10.3. Funerary inscriptions. These texts comprise the largest body of inscriptions from the ancient world. The earliest of these inscriptions, as Klaffenbach (1957:54) points out, occur on cliffs, whereas flat stone grave markers and stelae become the norm later on.

The earlier epitaphs contain one or two lines which tend to become longer and more complex during the classical period. Woodhead (1981: 44-5) lists the basic funerary formulas: ' "here lies...", "this is the tomb of...", "A set up this monument over B", "I am the tomb of B..." '. The simplest inscriptions contain only the name of the deceased with perhaps a patronymic and demotic. A descriptive adjective may be added to a man's name, but Woodhead says only rarely before the 3rd century. Women's epitaphs often record familial relationships but, as Klaffenbach (1957:56) states, the designation of familial relationships in the case of men is rare. If the name of the deceased occurs alone on a grave marker, it occurs in the nominative or genitive case. The genitive indicates the ownership of the grave (Klaffenbach 1957:55). The deceased's name rarely appears in the dative case. The names which appear on grave markers are single names until Roman times when the Roman practice of using cognomens is introduced. Injunctions against desecration of graves may also be added to inscriptions (Klaffenbach 1957:55; Woodhead 1981:45).

2.10.4. Miscellaneous. This class forms a body of inscriptions which deal with the average man on the street. Inscriptions of this type may consist simply of names, or lists of names, and, as Woodhead says, they tell us nothing more about these people than that they existed. Other inscriptions include boundary stones which mark off private or public property, mortgage stones, vases, inscriptions on small objects which often indicate ownership, and graffiti.

2.11. Summary

The preceding pages represent an attempt to show the diversity of the Greek alphabet not for the sake of Greek epigraphy per se but rather in order to shed light on the study of the runes and their origin. Runologists who have sought the origin of the runes in the Greek epigraphic alphabet have dealt not with an alphabet, which I have described in the preceding pages, nor with the epichoric varieties of that alphabet, but rather with one set, standard, and stylized Greek alphabet – the classical, Attic alphabet described in 2.1. This alphabet, which became the standard through a political act, is more or less the Greek alpahabet which was known and used through the early centuries of our era. The establishment of a standard alphabet, however, in no way precluded the use of

81

2. Greek Epigraphy

local alphabets in the Greek-speaking world, much in the same way that the introduction of the Latin alphabet in Scandinavia did not preclude the use of the runic alphabet. Little mention has been made among runologists of variant Greek letter forms, such as tailed *rho* R , crooked *iota* Ƨ , double-barred or boxed *heta* Ⱶ Ꮂ . Nor does it appear to be common knowledge among runologists that Greek *digamma* Ⅎ represented the semivowel /w/. Hammarström (1928) did mention some of these features of the Greek alphabet in relation to the runes but quickly dismissed them as too old to have any bearing on the runic alphabet. Others who mentioned these features (e.g. Hempl 1899, Kabell 1967) had no impact on discussion concerning the origin of the runic alphabet.

Runologists have also made few attempts at examining the role which phonology played in the borrowing of the runes. To this end I have briefly discussed some aspects of Greek phonology so that the runologist unfamiliar with Greek may have a point of reference during this investigation.

I have also discussed the direction of writing in Greek for the purpose of ascertaining whether a certain direction in writing can serve to indicate an inscription's age. It would seem that the answer is no. Even though one style may predominate in a certain period, it does not preclude others. Ernst Zinn (1950) implies that it was simply by chance that the Greeks settled on the direction left to right.

Such practices as the use of ligatures and various interpuncts in Greek epigraphic texts can also be seen in runic epigraphy. Whether or not they are remnants of Greek practice is a question which I shall take up later. The methods which the Greeks employed to prepare and execute a text may later shed some light on the preparation and execution of runic texts.

I will next proceed to a discussion of the Latin alphabet, paralleling the Greek alphabet. The purpose will again be to examine epigraphic forms and practices in order to be able to determine later what connections, if any, there may be between the Latin and runic alphabets.

3. LATIN EPIGRAPHY

3.1. The Latin alphabet: Background

The Latin alphabet derives ultimately, as do the modern European scripts, from the Greek alphabet. Its development and history differed from that of the Greek in that the Latin alphabet lacks the epichoric variation of the Greek. The oldest Latin inscription is found probably on the Forum cippus and stems from the 6th century. This dating leads scholars to posit the 8th century as the earliest date for the Latin alphabet. Of course in this time period there exists the problem of whether we are dealing with a Latin or Greek alphabet since the earliest Latin letter forms bear a striking resemblance to the Greek alphabet.

In its earliest stages, the Latin alphabet retained Greek symbols which, if not in the 8th century, were by the time of the Republic definitely obsolete. Latin retained Gk. *digamma* Ⅎ as a semivowel, Gk. *qoppa* Ϙ before *u* and *o*, Gk. *heta* H as an aspiration sign, and Gk. *zeta* Ⅰ in its Greek value /z/ (see Limentani 1974:145). In time, Gk. *digamma* came to stand for /f/, while Lat. *u* V came to designate /u/ as well as /w/. The Greek graph Ⅰ *zeta* as such was formally abolished in the year 312 B.C. by the censor Appius Claudius Caecus. In this same period the letter *g* G was invented to designate /g/, which had formerly been represented by Lat. *c* C. In archaic times, the Latin letter C from Gk. *gamma* < stood for both /k/ and /g/, which for Romans necessarily caused confusion due to the phonemic status of both /k/ and /g/. The Romans remedied this situation by adding an additional stroke to C to yield G. This new letter was then inserted in the Latin alphabet in *zeta's* place, where it remains until today. Gk. *chi* X was the only one of the Greek aspirates which was transmitted to the Latin alphabet. The value of Lat. X, however, was /ks/, which leads scholars to believe that it was a western Greek alphabet (Kirchhoff's red) in which X also had this value, that served as the mother of the Latin alphabet (Meyer 1973:23). Other graphic evidence which points towards a western Greek alphabet consists of Latin tailed *r* R , Lat. *h* H as a graph representing aspiration, and the Lat. *d* D (Calderini 1974:62).

The letters Y and Z (this letter not to be confused with the earlier form of Gk. *zeta* I , out of which Lat. Z did not develop) were added to the Latin alphabet in the penultimate and the ultimate places during the 2nd century before Christ to accommodate Greek spellings in Latin. With this latest addition to the Latin alphabet in the 2nd century before Christ, we have the alphabet in the order and form, except for *j* and *w*, in which it is known to us today.

3.2. *The origin of the Latin alphabet: Greek or Etruscan?*

From the previous section (3.1) one might hae the impression that the question of the Latin alphabet's origin has been settled. Ernst Meyer (1973:24) writes that the Etruscan transmission of the Greek alphabet to the Latins may be considered as proven. Not everyone, however, seems to be as convinced as Meyer. Aristide Limentani (1974:62; first edition 1967) writes that 'l'alfabeto latino è certo derivato da quello greco e quasi certamente dall'alfabeto calcidese di Cuma...pare certo che non vi sia stata una mediazione etrusca come alcuni hanno supposto, pur ammentendo influssi etruschi sulla scrittura latina'. The debate over just how the Romans got their alphabet, and from whom, has been going on since the days of the Romans themselves – even longer than the debate over the runes' origin. As Arthur E. Gordon (1969) has summarized and presented both sides of this argument, I will only briefly outline some of the major features of this debate.

One of the major points which speaks in favor of an Etruscan parentage for the Latin alphabet is that Lat. C derives ultimately from Gk. *gamma* < . The curious situation of how Gk. *gamma,* itself a voiced palatal stop, came to represent a voiceless palatal stop in its Latin form C has led scholars to believe that the Latin alphabet was trans-

3.2. The origin of the Latin alphabet: Greek or Etruscan?

mitted to the Romans via Etruria and the Etruscans. Meyer (1973:24 has this to say in favor of the Etruscan theory:

> Dafür sprechen insbesondere einige Besonderheiten in der Verwendung einzelner Buchstaben, die bei unmittelbarer Übernahme aus dem Griechischen schlecht erklärbar wären, aber in den Laurtverhältnissen des Etruskischen begründet sind, wie vor allem die Verwendung des griechischen Zeichens für g (gamma), lateinisch c, sowohl für g wie für k, aber später und so literarisch nur für k. Ebenso hat die lateinische Schrift Buchstaben des griechischen Alphabets nicht übernommen, die im etruskischen Schreibgebrauch fortgelassen waren, im Lateinischen als unentbehrlich nachträglich wieder neu gebildet wurden wie das g, das als Sonderform aus dem c entwickelt wurde.

Meyer refers here to the lack of voiced stops in the Etruscan sound system when he speaks of the 'Lautverhältnisse des Etruskischen'. Because of this lack, a graph in Greek which represented a voiced stop came to be a graph in Latin which represented a voiceless stop.

Other major points are discussed by Rhys Carpenter (1945:460). He notes that Gk. *qoppa* ϙ , which in Greek was used before *o* and *u*, is used in Latin only before *u*. Such a use of Gk. *qoppa* can be related to Etruscan alphabets which never used the letter *o*. Carpenter, however, notes an exception to this statement when he points out that the Duenos inscription shows ϙOI *QOI* 'qui' (6th century; see Figure 15).

One other issue which Carpenter brings up is that Latin letter names totally abandon the Greek, and with it the Semitic, nomenclature. Compare Gk. *alpha, beta, gamma*, etc. with Lat. *a, be, ce*, etc. Carpenter (1945:460) states:

> that this departure was due to Etruscan mediation may be claimed on the theory that there were sonant liquids and

nasals ("vocalic" *l*, *r*, etc.), in Etruscan speech and that these are reflected in the distinction which we still make today when we vocalize the letternames for *L, M, N, R,* and *S* as closed syllables ("ell," "em," etc.) although otherwise we regularly use open syllables for the consonants ("bee," "dee," "kay," etc.). There is no apparent reason why the Romans should have invented such a distinction.

(see also Hammarström 1920)

Critics of an Etruscan parentage for the Latin alphabet argue that if Etruscan did not use the graph *o*, nor the letters *b* and *d*, because voiced stops were lacking, then the Romans must have gotten these letters directly from the Greeks, of which there were many living on the Italian peninsula (see Gordon 1969). The letter *o* undoubtedly existed in the alphabet which the Etruscans learned from the Greeks, but whether the phoneme /o/ ever existed in Etruscan is doubted (see Pfiffig 1969: 28-9). The existence of /b, d, g/ is even more doubtful (see Pfiffig 1969: 36-8). Here, I might ask if the Etruscans did not use the letters *o, b, d,* then how could the Etruscans transmit these graphs to the Romans in the phonological value for which the Romans used them?

3.3. Latin letter forms

Although some points concerning the history of the Latin alphabet have been covered in preceding sections, this section will devote itself primarily to the forms of the letters at given points in time. Table 4 (Sandys 1969:48) shows the Latin alphabet in 3 separate periods. Column 1 shows the Latin alphabet with the letter forms that predominate in the years 279-254 B.C.; column 2, 253-154 B.C.; and column 3, 154 B.C. onwards. Table 4 does not include the letters Y and Z , which were borrowed from the Greek alphabet to accommodate Greek names and loanwords in Latin (see 3.1). The letter forms in column 1 also represent letter forms (with minor exceptions prior to 279 B.C. The letters *e, h, q,*

3.3. Latin letter forms

and *r* show slightly variant forms in the oldest inscriptions. The letter *e* shows a form ⋔ , with a slightly longer staff and with branches tilted downwards as on the Forum cippus inscription (Figure 14). The Forum cippus also shows boxed *h* ⊟ . The letter *q* has the form ♀ in the oldest inscriptions, as on the Forum cippus (Figure 14) and an inscribed beaker (Figure 13). The oldest forms of Lat. *r* P are tailless as on the Forum cippus. Lat. *z* I (≠ Z ; see 3.1) is inscriptionally attested in the Duenos inscription (Figure 15).

Of special interest are some of the older forms of the Latin letters represented in columns 1 and 2.

The following comments on Latin letter forms are taken from Sandys (1969:47-53), whose comments are more detailed than Limentani's (1973). Vittore Pisani (1957) also has a table of letter forms for alphabets of the Italic peninsula which is more detailed than Sandys's. Although Pisani's table includes alphabets other than Latin and while the overview of these Italic as well as non-Italic graph systems is remarkable, his table would give rise to unnecessary confusion for our purposes.

While Lat. *a, b,* and *c* are represented in table 4 and require no further comment, Lat. *d* shows more angular forms in older inscriptions, e.g. ▷ , Ð . The letters *e* and *f* typically have their branches deflected upwards E , F or downwards Ɛ , ꟼ in older inscriptions. These two letters also have secondary forms, *e* || and *f* |' . The letter *l* Ʋ typically has its lower branch angled upwards. The letters *m* ᴧᴧ and *n* ᴫ are closer to the Greek forms, while *m* ᶭ in the Forum inscription (Figure 14) looks more like the archaic Gk. *m* ᶭᴧ than the later classical Lat. M . The *o* ◇ , ◠ is typically not closed at the bottom in comparison to the classical *o* O , and it is often smaller than other letters in a given inscription. Other archaic forms of *o* are ( ) and ⟨ ⟩ . The pocket of Lat. *p* Γ is typically not closed in older inscriptions and looks more like Gk. *pi*. It is not until 100 A.D. that the forms of *p* P with a completely closed pocket are found. Lat. *r* R typically has a shorter tail than the form R during the Empire.

3. Latin Epigraphy

Table 4: Archaic Latin letter forms (Sandys 1969:48)

1	2	3
A ∧ ∧	A ∧	A
B B	B	B
< C	C	C
D	D	D
E E ‖	E ‖	E
F F I'	F I'	F
	G	G
H	H	H
I	I	I
K F	K	K
V	V L	L
∧ Ν	ΝΛ∧	M
Ν Ν	Ν N	N
◊ O Ω	O	O
Γ P	P P	P
? Q	Q	Q
R R	R	R
ƽ S	S	S
T	T	T
V	V	V
X	X	X

Column 1: 279-254 B.C.
Column 2: 253-154 B.C.
Column 3: 153 B.C. onwards

3.4. Latin inscriptions

The letter s ⟨ S , $\mathsf{\xi}$, $\mathsf{\}}$ ⟩ is often more angular than in the classical rounded forms.

Throughout the development of the Latin alphabet, the trend has been towards a more balanced, rectangular shape which no doubt is owing to the tools used in making inscriptions. By comparison, the earlier forms from the 6th to the 4th centuries look more like Greek, but in comparison with the Greek alphabet, Latin was much more uniform.

3.4. Latin inscriptions

The following inscriptions are intended to illustrate the letter forms which I have just discussed as well as to show the reader what the inscriptions looked like. The inscriptions are transliterated below the illustration. For the standard classical Latin text, the reader is referred to the *Corpus Inscriptionum Latinarum* (CIL). All transliterations are taken from CIL.

3.4.1. Beaker inscription (Figure 13). This inscription (CIL 1^2 no. 474) is found on the bottom of a beaker. Despite the fact that q is not supposed to be used before o (see 3.2.), we find the combination qo. The o's in this inscription are smaller than the other letters and the s ⟨ $\mathsf{\}}$ ⟩ has three crooks.

Figure 13: Beaker inscription (CIL 1^2 no. 474) *eqo K. Anaios*

3. Latin Epigraphy

3.4.2. The Forum cippus (Figure 14). The Forum cippus (CIL 1[2] no. 1) is a 6th century inscription which was found in the Roman Forum. The inscription runs boustrophedon on 4 sides of the stone. Lines 7-10 and 15-16 read in false boustrophedon (see 2.4.). The forms of the letters are again more reminiscent of Greek than of Latin.

3.4.3. Duenos inscription (Figure 15). The Duenos inscription (CIL 1[2] no. 4) runs from right to left around the outer edge of three vases which have been joined together. It was found near the Quirinal, one of the seven hills of Rome, and is dated to the early part of the 4th century. To my knowledge, this is the only inscription in Latin which shows Gk. *zeta* before it was officially eliminated from the Latin alphabet.

3.5. The Latin letters and their values

Table 5 shows the Latin alphabet and the phonological value of the letters in the 6th and 3rd centuries before Christ. I have not chosen the same centuries as I did for the Greek alphabet (see 2.3), i.e. the 8th and 4th centuries, because the Latin alphabet is not as old as the Greek. I also want to show the phonological values of the Latin letters in their earliest attestation and in the period when the Latin alphabet underwent its standardizing reforms (see 3.1). A quick glance at table 5 reveals that there have been no major changes in the phonological value of the letters from the 6th to the 3rd centuries. In fact there is very little change in this system until the late Empire. Changes in the phonological value of letters, such as in Gk. *(h)eta* from /h/ to /e/ because of the loss of initial /h/, did not occur in Latin. The names of the latin letters were a syllabic realization of the letter itself plus a vowel, e.g. *b* plus *e* resulted in *be*. The phonological values of the letters alone do not depend on the environment. For example, *n* would still be called *en* regardless of whether or not it is pronouned in the word *consul*. On the other hand, Gk. **H** would always be called *eta* once initial /h/ has been lost. Although positional variants may have existed, as in the case of final *m* (see 3.6.1),

90

3.5. The Latin letters and their values

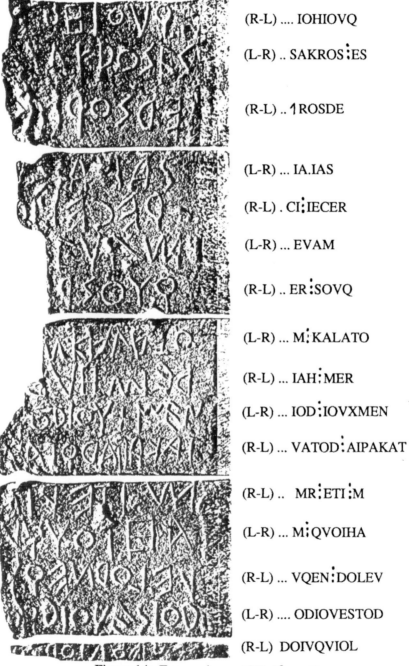

(R-L) .... IOHIOVQ

(L-R) .. SAKROS⋮ES

(R-L) .. ꟼROSDE

(L-R) ... IA.IAS

(R-L) . CI⋮IECER

(L-R) ... EVAM

(R-L) .. ER⋮SOVQ

(L-R) ... M⋮KALATO

(R-L) ... IAH⋮MER

(L-R) ... IOD⋮IOVXMEN

(R-L) ... VATOD⋮AIPAKAT

(R-L) .. MR⋮ETI⋮M

(L-R) ... M⋮QVOIHA

(R-L) ... VQEN⋮DOLEV

(L-R) .... ODIOVESTOD

(R-L) DOIVQVIOL

Figure 14: Forum cippus (CIL 1² no. 1)

91

3. Latin Epigraphy

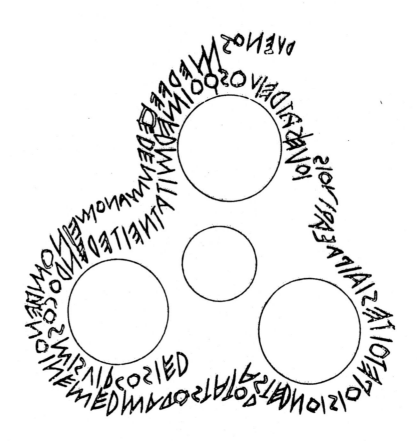

Figure 15: Duenos inscription (CIL 1² no. 4)

Line 1: *iovesatdeivosqoimedmitatneitedendocosmisvircosied*

Line 2: *astednoisiopetoitesiaipacarivois*

Line 3: *dvenosmedfecedenmanomeinomdzenoinemedma(n)ostatod*

92

3.5. The Latin letters and their values

Table 5: Latin letter/sound correspondence

Letter	Sound value 6th century	Sound value 3rd century
A	a	a
B	b	b
C	k, g	k
D	d	d
E	e	e
F	w, f	f
G	---	g
H	h	h
I	i (j)	i (j)
K	k (before a)	k*
L	l	l
M	m	m
N	n	n
O	o	o
P	p	p
Q	k	ku̯ (QV)
R	r	r
S	s	s
T	t	t
V	u (w)	u (w)
X	ks	ks
Y	---	y**
Z	---	z**

* only used in certain words and abbreviations
** for Greek words

they did not phonemically effect the phonological value of a letter in isolation.

The Latin vowels /a, e, i, o, u/ were written respectively with the letters A , E (II), I , O , V without consideration of length. The vowel graph Y y was borrowed from Greek and used only for Greek loan words (Sturtevant 1940:122).

The Latin semivowels [j] and [w] were positional variants of /i/ and /u/ and as such were written with the vowel graphs I and V . In the earliest times, however, Lat. [w] was also written with F from Gk. *digamma* Γ . This usage of *digamma* was given up at a very early time in Rome (Sturtevant 1940:140; Limentani 1974:145).

The Latin voiced stops /b, d, g/ were represented by the letters B , D , G . As pointed out earlier (3.1), however, the letter G was derived from C in the 3rd century. Prior to this time, /g/ was written as C and occasionally Ϙ q (see Figure 13). A remnant of expressing /g/ with C can be seen in the abbreviations C for *Gaius* and CN for *Gnaeus* (Meyer 1973:33).

The Latin voiceless stops /p, t, k/ were written as P (Γ), T , and C or K (Ⅎ). The letter C was originally used before *i* and *e*, and K only before *a*. This non-phonemic distinction in the orthography was done away with by the 3rd century and the letter K remains only in isolated words, e.g. *kalendae, kandidatus, Volkanus* (Meyer 1973:33).

The Latin digraph Q V represented a voiceless velar stop with lip-rounding [kʷ] (Sturtevant 1940:169-70).

The Latin letter H was a sign of aspiration [h]. Sturtevant (1940: 155-60] indicates that Lat. *h* may have been [x] at a very early stage of Latin but 'from the time of our earliest documents, Lat. *h* was an unstable sound'. He also remarks that the correct use of Lat. *h* was a mark of social distinction. Lat. *h* was lost between like vowels, after consonants, and it never prevented elision. Furthermore, Sturtevant remarks that the Roman grammarians connected Lat. *h* with Attic rough breathing and that they themselves called it *aspiratio*. The great influx of Greek words into Latin influenced the usage of Lat. *h*. The Romans

94

transliterated the Greek aspirates Φ, Θ, X, with *ph, th,* and *ch* and overzealous Romans soon began to introdue *h* into Greek words where it did not belong. They then began introducing *h* into Latin words after *c, p,* and *t.*

Latin also had a labio-dental spirant /f/ which was written F .

The Latin resonants /l, r, m, n/ were regularly written with L , R , M , and N .

3.6. Latin orthographic practices

Orthographic practices which are particular to Latin epigraphy are the treatment of nasals (3.6.1), the doubling of letters to indicate length (3.6. 2), the invention of letters and diacritics to represent certain phonological features (3.6.3), and the use of single consonants to stand for entire syllables (3.6.4).

3.6.1. Treatment of nasals. The treatment of nasals in Latin epigraphy is especially relevant to runic studies because of the statements made by Makaev (1965:58) regarding the ommission of nasals in runic inscriptions (see 4.4.1) and a possible parallel practice in Greek (see 2.4). If a similar practice were to be found in one of the Mediterranean epigraphic traditions, then this would demonstrate a much closer relationship between the runes and a Mediterranean alphabet than has heretofore been admitted.

In Latin epigraphy, there does exist an orthographic practice of not representing the letter *n* before *s.* This nonrepresentation of *n* before *s* dates back to the earliest inscriptions and is attested in such words as COSUL *consul* and CESOR *censor.* This orthographic practice reflects a change in Latin whereby *n* before V̆_s becomes Ṽ̄s. The *n* was no longer perceived to be a consonant and therefore was not written (Sturtevant 1940:153-4). This orthographic practice, however, was not consistent because certain words and abbreviations were normally written without *n,* especially COS *consul,* while other words could be written

95

3. Latin Epigraphy

either way, e.g. LIBES versus LIBENS and MESES versus MENSES (Meyer 1973:34). This orthographic practice which reflects the above-mentioned phonological development is specific to the environment V̌_s for, as Sturtevant (1940:154) notes, 'there is no tendency in pre-classical or clsssical times to omit *n* in the group *nf* even though lengthening of the preceding vowel does occur'.

A doubt whether final *m* in Latin inscriptions represents [m] or nasalization of the preceding vowel does exist. As evidence for the status of final *m*, Sturtevant (1940:151-3) cites Quintilian, a Latin grammarian of the 1st century after Christ, who says:

> Atqui eadem illa littera, quotiens ultima est et vocalem verbi sequentis ita contingit ut in eam transire possit, etiamsi scri-bitur, tamen parum exprimitur, ut *multum ille* et *quantum erat;* adeo ut paene cuisdam novae litterae sonum reddat. Neque enim eximitur sed obscuratur et tantum aliqua inter duas vocales velut nota est ne ipsae coeant.

Whether final *m* was pronounced or not, is not of such great concern here as is the matter of its orthographic treatment in inscriptions. Inter-estingly enough, however, this weakening or loss of final *m* is demon-strated in an inscription from the year 259 B.C. (CIL 1^2 no. 2)

HONC OINO PLOIRUME CONSENTIONT R[...]//
DUONORO OPTUMO FUISE VIRO
Hunc unum plurimae consentiunt R[...]//
virum bonorum optimum fuisse

Also of interest in this inscription are the words CONSOL and CENSOR which appear 2 lines further down with the *n*'s.

The case where *n* before *s* is not designated in writing seems to result from phonemic indeterminancy conditioned by a given phonologi-cal environment. The case of final *m*, however, may be governed more

3.6. Latin orthographic practices

by the sandhi-rules of Latin where *m* comes under weak stress and is not pronounced. As no other types of nondesignation of nasals seem to exist, it appears that this orthographic practice is limited to these two cases.

3.6.2. Doubling of letters to indicate length. The practice of doubling consonants and vowels to indicate length is traditionally traced back to two poets – Ennius (239-169 B.C.) for consonant doubling and Accius (ca. 170-85 B.C.) for vowel doubling.

The earliest known example of double consonants appears on an inscription from 211 B.C. Warmington (1940:4.76) indicates that this inscription HINNAD is a transliteration of Gk. Ἔννα. However, the earliest known native Latin example of consonant doubling to indicate length is found in a decree (CIL 1² no. 5041) from 189 B.C. This inscription shows the form POSSIDERE. The use of double consonants, however, seems to have been inconsistent as evidenced by another form of the same word in the same inscription, POSEDISSENT (Sandys 1969:36). Sandys indicates that double consonants become common by 100 B.C. Although writing double consonants becomes normal Latin usage, Warmington (1940:4.xx-xxi) reports that in the period from 175 to 135 B.C. instances of doubling equal instances of writing consonants singly. From 115 B.C. on, double consonants become the norm, but instances of single consonants also occur.

The writing of double vowels to indicate long vowels was a short-lived practice even though, as Meyer (1973:34) indicates, isolated instances are found during the Empire. Sandys (1969:36) states that instances of this practice are found in the period from 133. B.C. to 75 B.C. Revilo Oliver (1966:152) holds this practice to be an imitation of Oscan even though it is traditionally ascribed to Accius. This practice, however, is superseded by the use of an accent mark, the apex (see 3.6.3).

3.6.3. Special letters and diacritics. Among the graphs to be discussed in this section are inverted digamma, antisigma, half-aspirate ('mezza

3. Latin Epigraphy

aspirazione'), tall-*i* *(i-longa), apex,* and *sicilicus.*

The inverted digamma, antisigma, and half-aspirate were invented by the Emperor Claudius in the 1st century after Christ. They were implemented by decree and lasted no longer than Claudius's reign (Limentani 1974:146). Inverted digamma ⅃ represented /w/; antisigma Ɔ , /ps/ or /bs/; and the half-aspirate Ⱶ , /y/. Only inverted digamma and the half-aspirate are attested in inscriptions (Meyer 1973:28).

Tall-*i* | , that is an *i* extending above the other letters, first appears at the end of the 2nd century before Christ and is often used to indicate /ī/. Writing tall-*i* for /ī/ becomes common practice. Meyer (1973: 35-6), however, points out, 'doch gibt es genügend Fälle, wo auch kurzes i mit i-longa geschrieben wird anscheinend aus rein graphisch-dekorativen Gründen'.

The *apex* and *sicilicus* were diacritic marks used to indicate length of vowels and consonants (Sandys 1969:53). The apex was an accent-like mark ˃ , or during the Empire ´ , placed over vowels to show length. The oldest evidence appears on an inscription from the year 104 BC. (Meyer 1973:34). This mark is very common in the Empire, but as Meyer states, the *apex* is never used consistently. the *sicilicus* is a sickle-like mark which in its oldest form ˃ is identical to the *apex* (Meyer 1973:35). This diacritic was placed above consonants to indicate doubling.

3.6.4. Single consonants standing for entire syllables. Another orthographic practice in pre-Imperial Latin inscriptions, is the deletion or nonrepresentation of *e* or *a* in certain syllables. In such cases the initial consonant stands for the entire syllable. As A.Grenier (1924:40) said, 'on sait que l'ancienne épigraphie latine supprime parfois la voyelle entre deux consonnes; il faut alors, pour lire le mot, prononcer non pas le son, mais le nom de la première consonne; *bne* par example, se lira *bene, dcimus, decimus; krus, karus'.* This practice is thought to be related to Etruscan practice and the names of the letters in Latin (see Ernout 1905:307-15). The convention is attested in inscriptions from the entire Italic peninsula in the period before the Empire (see Ernout 1905).

3.7. *Direction of writing*

The problem of direction in writing does not seem to be of as great a concern for epigraphists of Latin as it is for those of Greek (see 2.5). We find the direction right-to-left in the oldest inscriptions, e.g. the Duenos inscription (Figure 15), as well as boustrophedon, e.g. on the Forum cippus (Figure 14), which is of the type which Jeffery (1961:49-50) would classify as false boustrophedon (see 2.5). Instances of right-to-left writing and boustrophedon are isolated in the earliest inscriptions and they become even rarer as time progresses. Left-to-right writing quickly became the standard (Meyer 1973: 37) and it seems that this happened very early in Latin, almost to the exclusion of other directions (see also Limentani 1974:152).

3.8. *Ligatures*

Ligatures, the combination of letters into one graph, was also known in Rome during the pre-classical period. They first appear, according to Battle-Huguet (1963:17) and Sandys (1969:53), around 200 B.C. on coins and around 150 B.C. on monuments. In addition to forming ligatures by having individual letters share a common staff, e.g. Ꝑ *ab,* ⋀ *na,* ⋁ *va,* ⋈ *nth,* one letter may be inscribed inside another, e.g. Ⓐ *ca,* Ⓖ *go,* Ⓠ *qv.* Problems may arise in reading Latin ligatures because the letters of a ligature may be read in varying orders. For example, ᵱ may be read *eb* or *be* (Calderini 1974:72). Although the examples presented here may seem sparse, they abound in the handbooks. I refer the reader to René Cagnat (1914:24-6), who drew up one of the first comprehensive tables of Latin ligatures. These have been reproduced by Battle-Huguet (1963:18-21) and Calderini (1974:71-3).

3. Latin Epigraphy

3.9. Abbreviations

Abbreviations in Latin epigraphy abound throughout the history of the Latin alphabet. As Calderini (1974:69) states, abbreviations occupy an important position in Latin epigraphy. They occur most frequently with names ('praenomina'), titles, and the more common words or stock phrases, e.g. C *Gaius,* F *filius,* M̂ *Marcus,* COS *consul,* F̂ *fecit,* I D Q *idemque,* PQ *populusque,* D̄ N̄ *dominus noster* (Limentani 1973:150-1; Calderini 1974:69-71). To indicate plurals, certain key letters of the abbreviation are repeated as many times as necessary to indicate the number, e.g. DDDD NNNN *domini nostri quattor* (Calderini 1974:70). With certain abbreviations, such as C *Gaius* and F *filius,* the feminine counterpart may be indicated by reversing the letter, e.g. Ɔ *Gaia,* ⅂ *femina.* For more comprehensive lists of examples, I refer the reader to Calderini (1974:70).

3.10. Interpunction

Interpuncts used in Latin inscriptions vary from two or three dots arranged vertically, ⁚ , ⁚ , to one dot ˙ , a leaf ✿ , a small triangle, or spacing (Limentani 1974:149-50; Meyer 1973:36-7). The oldest inscriptions, according to Meyer, favor the use of dots, while late Republican inscriptions favor small triangles as well as more decorative symbols. The interpuncts, however, do not seem to be employed according to a regular rule, but they are there and in large numbers. In comparison to Greek inscriptions, spacing of the use of interpuncts is widely employed in Latin: 'Im Gegensatz zu den griechischen Inscrhriften, die ohne Worttrennung schreiben, herrscht in lateinischen Inschriften das Prinzip der Worttrennung, und zwar vor allem durch besondere Worttrenner' (Meyer 1973:36). If no interpuncts were used, the words still tend to be separated: 'Le parole sono tra loro spaziate; molto spesso tra una e l'altra era posto un segno separativo, in iscrizioni arcaiche formato anche da due o tre puntini allineati in verticale' (Limentani 1974:149).

100

3.11. Preparation and layout of the text; epigraphic material

The process(es) involved in preparing a text for inscription as well as its arrangement and technical execution are the same for latin as Greek (2. 8) with some minor exceptions (see Susini 1973; Meyer 1973:20-2). Most inscriptions were made in workshops where an apparent division of labor existed. Although the problem of the exact division of labor in preparing and executing a text as well as of the Latin terminology for these processes is not resolved, the various Latin words which deal with epigraphy, e.g. *ordinator, lapidarius, ordinatio, scribere, sculpere,* clearly show that some division of labor must have occurred in these workshops.

Meyer is of the opinion that official or longer private inscriptions were first written out and later transferred to stone, whereas most shorter private inscriptions were probably given to the workshops orally. The craftsmen in these shops then fit the information into their stock phrases.

The writing surface of a stone would often be polished before being written upon. In contrast to the Greeks, who would very often polish all sides of a stone, even if they were not to be used, the Romans would only polish or smooth out that particular areas where the inscription would stand, the *titulus* (Susini 1973:22). The next step was to scratch in guidelines on the *titulus* on which the letters would then be sketched out. These guidelines could at times be drawn in with paint or chalked on with a taught string. After the guidelines had been set up, the letters were first drawn or painted on and then chiseled in.

Errors which occur in Latin inscriptions can be traced, as Susini (1973:39-49) indicates, to several sources. Perhaps the person sketching the inscription on the stone misread the handwritten draft; the person arranging the text on the stone left something out; the person chiseling in the letter was careless and either executed the wrong letter or just began to execute the wrong letter. Some examples which Susini (1973:41) gives are: *STVRORE* for *STVPORE, ASEENDEVA* for *ASCENDEVA, NACQE* for *NACQVE,* and *ERNIS* corrected to *ERONIS* by squeezling the *o* in between the *r* and the *n.*

101

3. Latin Epigraphy

Additions could be made between lines or at the end of the text. Additions to a text could reflect either omissions on the part of the craftsman, e.g. *ERNIS* and *ERONIS,* or an afterthought on the part of the customer who ordered the work and then decided to have something added.

The epigraphic materials used by the Romans correspond to those used by the Greeks. In other words, they wrote on anything. However, the greatest number of inscriptions occur on stone, be it an individual stone, a statue, the wall of a building, or the side of a cliff (Meyer 1973: 17-9). The second greatest number of inscriptions occurs on bronze tablets. Inscriptions also occur on clay tablets, pottery, jewelry, weapons, to name but a few.

3.12. *Types of inscriptions*

Latin inscriptions can be divided into six major categories (Sandys 1969; Battle-Huguet 1963): dedications (3.12.1), honorary inscriptions (3.12.2), funerary inscriptions (3.12.3), inscriptions on public works, public and private acts, and miscellaneous (3.12.4). The categories 'inscriptions on public works' as well as 'public and private acts' will not be discussed because they would have no bearing on runic studies. These two categories consist of laws, plebiscites, public decrees, building dedications, roadside milestones, etc. (see Battle-Huguet 1963:81-91). I have tried to maintain a balance between this section and the Greek section (2.10). The differences between these two sections reflect a difference in their treatment in the handbooks rather than in the inscriptions themselves.

3.12.1. Dedications. Dedicatory inscriptions *(tituli sacri)* concern themselves with dedications of objects to a deity. The oldest inscriptions in this class, as in the other classes, are short. At times, they simply contain the name of the deity in the genitive, which indicates ownership by the deity, or in the dative case, which expresses the idea of dedication. The occurrence of the name in the genitive case is not as frequent as its occurrence in the dative (Battle-Huguet 1963:78). The basic linguistic structure of the inscription is similar to the Greek (2.8.1). The dedicator appears in the nominative; the dedicatee in the dative or genitive; and the verb, almost always expressed, in the 1st or the 3rd person. Supplementary information may appear, such as the object dedicated in the accusative, additional names and titles of the dedicator in the nominative, and the reason for dedication.

3.12.2. Honorary inscriptions. Honorary inscriptions *(elogia)* were erected to honor a certain person for certain deeds. These inscriptions are most typical of Imperial Rome, beginning with Augustus (Battle-Huguet 1963:67) The oldest inscriptions are again short and become more elaborate as time goes on. The name of the person being honored as well as his charges appears in older inscriptions in the nominative case and later, after Sulla, in the dative (Sandys 1969:106). Some very early examples exist, however, where the name of the person honored appears in the accusative. Sandys (1969:94) attributes the use of the accusative to Greek practice, where the custom of setting up such inscriptions originated. The person or group bestowing the honor, as well as titles or relationship to the one honored, appears in the nominative. The verb is usually not expressed. When it is expressed, it follows the name of the bestower(s). The name of the bestower usually follows the reason for bestowal.

3.12.3. Funerary inscriptions. Funerary inscriptions are found overwhelmingly on stone. In the oldest inscriptions, only the name of the deceased appears in either the nominative or the genitive with no allusion to the person's death. In later inscriptions, around 250 B.C. (Sandys 1969:61), the deceased's profession is added and even later the deceased's age in the genitive case. Religious dedications were added in Augustus's reign. The inscriptions, as they become more elaborate, begin to contain information about the deceased's accomplishments, why the tomb was erected, familial relations, salutations to passers-by, and who raised the tomb (Battle-Huguet 1963:71-5; Sandys 1969:60-82).

3.12.4. Miscellaneous. Inscriptions included in this class (Battle-Huguet 1963:94-9; Sandys 1969:141-55) cover many aspects of Roman life. Industrial inscriptions contain information on the origin of the products, e.g. which mine a particular piece of marble came from. The *tesserae,* small pieces of metal, marble, lead, bone, or ivory, contain small pieces of information. The *tesserae militares* are Roman dog-tags; the *tesserae frumentariae* are a type of purchase order which entitled the bearer to pick up a certain quantity of goods; the *tesserae conviviales* are a type of admission ticket to a public function which often include numbers indicating which seat a person has.

Other inscriptions included in this class are those on jewelry such as rings, bracelets, and fibulae. This type usually contains the name of the owner and the weight of the jewel or silver. Phrases such as *amo te* 'I love you' and *uror amore tuo* 'I burn with love of you' are found in such inscriptions. As Battle-Huguet (1963:98) indicates, these items were given as tokens of love.

Other inscriptions in this class are those found on slave collars, spells, and graffiti (Battle-Huguet 1963:93-9).

3.13. Summary

The Latin alphabet from its very beginning lacked the epichoric character of the Greek alphabet. The forms of the letters in the Latin alphabet are relatively uniform throughout the Roman world. The only major differences between the alphabet of Rome proper and of Gaul and Germania are seen in the letters | | *e*, | ' *f,* and Đ *d.* By the birth of Christ, however, the Latin alphabet achieved the form in which it is known to us today (except for *j* and *w*).

Even before the writing reform of 312 B.C. by the censor Appius Claudius Caecus, the direction of writing had become standardized in Latin to left-to-right. Prior to this reform, only the oldest Latin inscriptions show a boustrophedon or right-to-left pattern.

Latin practice shows that nasals were not represented before *s,* and less frequently before *f*. This practice was motivated by the eventual phonological weakening and loss of *n* in that environment. The practice, however, was not uniform. Runologists have often maintained that runic Ⴡ can only come from Lat. Ⴡ *h*, but it seems that /h/ was lost very early in Latin and maintained artificially by 'schoolteachers' to the point that initial /h/ became hypercorrect. The influx of Greek words with rough breathing into Latin also helped to preserve Lat. *h* in the alphabet.

Prior to 189 B.C., there are no examples of double letters in Latin inscriptions. Afterwards, the usage of double letters began to increase until it became standard by the year 115 B.C. Special diacritics were used in Latin to indicate vowel and consonantal length, but not until the 1st century before Christ.

The Latin letter-names provide a remarkable phenomenon in that they are not really names at all. Unlike the Greek letter-names, the first sound of which indicated the value of that letter, the latin letter-names are simply the sounds of those letters, as in modern English, *a, bee, cee*, etc. The names of the consonants, the sound of that consonant plus *a* or *e*, enabled the Romans to use single consonants to stand for entire syllables – a type of abbreviation.

Ligatures first appear in Latin usage around 200 B.C. and became quite common by the 1st century before Christ, whereas abbreviations are known in Latin from the earliest inscriptions.

The preparation and execution of epigraphic texts followed much the same techniques as those used in Greek inscriptions. The types of inscriptions constitute relatively the same groups as in Greek. The Romans raised monuments to their heroes and public figures and set stones to commemorate the deceased. Moreover, they used the alphabet as common everyday tool for communication in trade, polical and military matters, and affairs of the heart.

I will next proceed to a discussion of runic epigraphy to show the similarities between it and the archaic Greek and Latin traditions.

4. RUNIC EPIGRAPHY

4.0. Introduction

The following chapter examines the runic tradition in light of the Greek and Latin traditions. Comparisons for similarities and dissimilarities among the three traditions will be made wherever possible. The comparisons, wherever possible, are limited to those inscriptions in the older fuþark (ca. 0 – 500 A.D.), while some examples are taken from the so-called transitional period (500 – ca. 700 A.D.). Because bibliographic information on any of the inscriptions may be obtained from any number of treatments (Jacobsen/Moltke 1941; Krause 1966; Antonsen 1975a; Høst 1976) and bibliographies (Marquardt 1961; Schnall 1973; Düwel 1983), I have restricted my references to only one or two sources. In most cases, I refer to Antonsen (1975a) because his readings and interpretations are linguistically sound, and to Krause (1966) because he gives background information on the inscriptions and reproductions of them. For inscriptions that have come to light since the compilation of the various corpus editions, I refer the reader to Moltke (1985) for high quality photographs of the inscriptions that he treats and to Stoklund (1986) for high quality photographs and a provocative treatment of the Illerup Ådal finds. Abbreviations used in this chapter are as follows: A = Antonsen 1975a; H = Høst 1976; K = Krause 1966; M = Moltke 1985.

4.1. The older runic alphabet

The older runic alphabet consists of a 24-letter series which is called the *fuþark* after the first six runes of the sequence. The fuþark is attested in its entirety in 2 inscriptions: the Kylver stone (K, no. 1) and the Vadstena bracteate (K, no. 2). The Kylver stone is depicted in figure 16. The

107

division of the fuþark into three families of 8 runes is seen on the Vadstena bracteate (Figure 17).

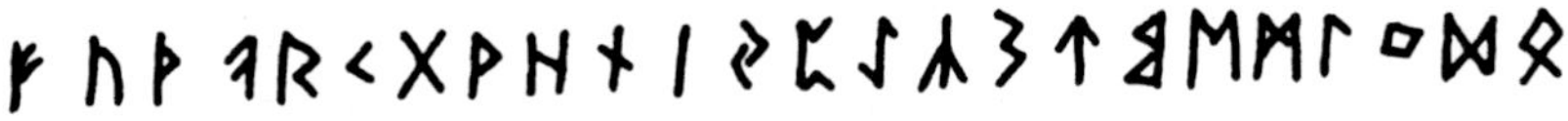

ᚠᚢᚦᚨᚱᚲᚷᚹᚺᚾᛁᛃᛈᛇᛉᛊᛏᛒᛖᛗᛚᛜᛞᛟ

f u þ a r k g w h n i j p æ z s t b e m l n͡g d o

Figure 16: Kylver fuþark

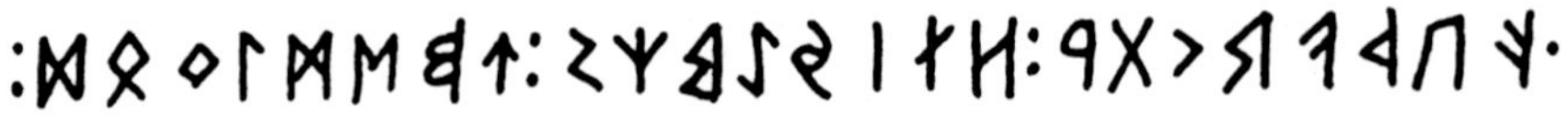

ᛞᛟᛜᛚᛗᛖᛒᛏᛊᛉᛈᛇᛃᛁᚾᚺᚹᚷᚲᚱᚨᚦᚢᚠ

d o n͡g l m e b t s z p æ j i n h w g k r a þ u f

Figure 17: Vadstena fuþark (R-L)

The order of the runes in these 2 fuþarks is the same except that the
Kylver fuþark shows the order ᛇ ᛈ ᛉ for runes 12-14, while the
Vadstena fuþark shows ᛇ ᛏ ᛒ (ᛒ for ᛈ); Kylver has ᛜ ᛟ for
runes 23-24, while Vadstena has ᛟ ᛜ . The order *d o* is confirmed for
the fuþark by the English Thames scramasax fuþorc (Page 1973:41).

   The remaining fuþarks are found on the Grumpan bracteate (K, no.
3), the Breza column (K, no. 5), the Lindkær bracteate (K, no. 4), the
Aquincum clasp (K, no. 7), the Charnay clasp (K, no. 6), and the
Beuchte clasp (K, no. 8), which all date from the 6th century after Christ.
These fuþarks are not complete; each contains only parts of the entire
24-rune sequence. The extant rune series attest to a set order within the
older runic alphabet, except for the Breza column which has the
sequence for runes 17-19, ᛏ ᛖ ᛜ. The *b*-rune which should come
after the *t*-rune is omitted. In addition, the later development of cryptic
runes (Engl. *hahal-runes*, Ger. *Zweigrunen*, Sw. *kvistrunor*) in the
younger fuþarks further attest to a uniform sequence in the older runes.
These cryptic runes consisted of a staff and branches on both sides of the
staff to indicate the family and which rune in that family was meant. For
example, a cryptic rune ᚹ indicated the fourth rune of the first family,

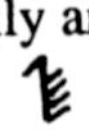

namely *a* (see Düwel 1983:96-101).

The order of the runes in the fuþark, as well as their names (4.8), does not correspond to any of the contemporary alphabets. This deviation on the part of the fuþark from the Mediterranean alphabets has long been a bane to runic scholars. It has led to speculations varying in range from the mystical (e.g. Jungandreas 1974) to the geometrical (e.g. Klingenberg 1973). Jens Jensen (1969) suggested that the runes were put in their order according to a symmetrical patterning of consonants and vowels. As is the case with the names of the runes, their order probably arose out of some mnemonic/conceptual device and the only tangible conclusion can be, as Arntz (1944:85) said, 'daß es sich aber um eine alte und allgemein germanische Entwicklung handelt, beweisen die Runenreihen, die mit überraschender Gleichheit immer wieder die [gleiche] Folge...zeigen'.

Linguistic developments within the Germanic languages later led to the development of the 16-rune younger fuþark in Scandinavia (ca. 800 A.D.; see Trnka 1939; Antonsen 1963; Rischel 1967; Haugen 1969; Liestøl 1981) and of the 31-rune English fuþorc (see Page 1973). As these younger runic systems are clearly later developments of the older 24-rune system, they do not fall within the scope of this discussion.

4.2. *The forms of the runes*

Rash generalizations, such as 'this form is older' or 'this form shows a development', have been made over the years regarding the shapes of the runes and their variants. In fact, it has become a tradition among runologists to presume a certain chronological development of letter shapes and then to use these criteria for dating inscriptions. Lis Jacobsen (1942: 1.935) wrote, 'Sandsynligheden taler for, at de kantede former er ældst'. Helmut Arntz (1944:66) wrote, ' ⋀ scheint uns die älteste Form der u-Rune, weil aus ihr die übrigen sich herleiten lassen: zunächst ⋀ aus dem Streben nach einem senkrechten Hauptstab, sodann ⋔ , ⋔ vielleicht durch Einfluß der r-Rune in der Form ⋉ '.

4. Runic Epigraphy

Moltke (1985:32) assumes a priori that runes were probably first written on wood with no horizontal lines and therefore that nonangular shapes in the runes are younger: 'It is therefore on metal and stone that we first meet runes that have horizontal or rounded lines. For this reason, too, it is obvious that the ng rune in the Kylver alphabet is not an original detail, nor is the e rune ∏ as opposed to M '. Among the oldest inscriptions however, are the Illerup Ådal spearhead and shield grip inscriptions that demonstrate both rounded and angular forms (Stoklund 1985).

Gerd Høst (1976:42) also assumes that letter shapes can help date an inscription, which in turn implies that rune shapes can be chronologically ordered. In reference to the Barmen stone, she writes, 'Barmeninnskriften dateres – særlig på grunn av j-runens gamle form [⟨⟩] – til første halvdel av 5. årh.'.

Such assumptions are difficult to prove when dealing with a corpus as limited as that of the older runes. Woodhead (1981:62) warns against such practice in Greek epigraphy, where the size of the corpus would statistically lend itself to such conclusions much more readily than the size of the runic corpus. When speaking of the Øvre Stabu spearhead (K, no. 31; A, no. I; H, 108), which is generally dated to the years 150-200 A.D., Krause states, 'der archäologische Befund weist nach den Untersuchungen von A. E. Hartig und von H. J. Eggers in den Anfang der jüngeren Kaiserzeit..., also in die zweite Hälfte des zweiten Jhs. Für diesen Ansatz spricht auch die altertümliche Form der j-Rune [↜]'. When later speaking of the Kalleby stone (K, no. 61), Krause makes a similar statement: 'Die Form der j-Rune [↜] weist auf hohes Alter, etwa um 400'.

The j-runes of these two inscriptions both show the same form ↜ , the former dated to 150-200 and the latter to 400 A.D. When discussing the Dahmsdorf spearhead (K, no. 32), which shows the j-rune as ⟨, Krause says, 'Die j-Rune hat die altertümliche Form'. In talking about the Skåäng stone (K, no. 85), which has the same form ⟨ , Krause mentions: 'Die Form der j-Rune scheint typologisch etwas jünger als die auf dem Stein von Stenstad', ca. 400 A.D. He then pro-

4.2. The forms of the runes

ceeds to date the Skåäng stone to 500 A.D. Krause has, however, described the *j* of the Dahmsdorf spearhead as 'altertümlich' and has dated this inscription to 250 A.D. One *j* is described as 'altertümlich' and the other as 'jünger' when they both seem to bear the same shape. I might point out that Krause's dating of the Skåäng inscriptions ca. 500 A.D. is beginning to approach the transitional period in the runic inscriptions marked by the use of the *(j)āra*-rune ✳ for /a/ after the loss of initial /j/, as seen in the Ellestad stone of Östergötland 550-600 A.D (A, no. 114), and the Setre comb 550-600 A.D. (A, no. 115; H, 69).

Table 6 is a representation of *j*-runes taken from inscriptions spanning the time from 150-550 A.D. This representation is not complete, as it does not represent every *j*-rune in the corpus of the older fuþark, but rather a sampling which should show the lack of a systematic, chronological development in the minor variations in the shape of the *j*-rune. To be noted, however, is the fact that each of these *j*-runes, regardless of the date, consists of two crooks (see 4.2.12). After examining table 6, it can be seen that if we should date an inscription on the basis of runic shapes, then the Øvre Stabu spearhead and the Gallehus gold horn 2 should not be separated by some 250 years, nor should the Thorsberg chapes and the Nordhuglo stone be separated by some 225 years.

A similar sampling of the *u*-rune is found in table 7. Krause (1966:2) proposed that the oldest form of the *u*-rune was Λ (see 4.2.2.). His dating, however, for the Årstad and Opedal stones does not reflect this view. Similarly, Krause's dating of the Højstrup bracteate should be much earlier, based on this criterion. It would seem then from these samplings of the *j*- and *u*-runes that Woodhead's admonishment for the epigraphists of Greek should also be directed towards runologist, i.e., that dating on the basis of letter shape is at best tenuous.

The attention given to the shapes of the runes and variant forms has lacked systematic analysis, which prompted Antonsen (1975a; 1979) to propose a system of graphemic analysis for the runes. He developed this system by comparing debatable runes within an individual inscription to clearly discernible ones, e.g. the *u*'s and the *r*'s on the Fyn brac-

111

Table 6: Forms of the *j*-rune

(The years indicated are agreed upon by both Antonsen and Krause. Where Krause's dating differs from Antonsen's, it will be noted. All dates are after Christ.)

Øvre Stabu spearhead	∿	150-200	(A, no. 1; K, no. 31)
Illerup Ådal spearheads	⟨	150-200	(Stoklund 1986)
Thorsberg chape	⟨⟩	200	(A, no. 2; K, no. 20)
Nøvling shieldboss	⟩	200	(A, no. 4; K, no. 13a)
Dahmsdorf spearhead	⟨⟩	250	(A, no. 7; K, no. 32)
Vimose comb	⟩⟨	250	(A, no. 8; K, no. 26)
Vimose woodplane	⟨⟩	250-300	(A, no. 10; K, no. 25)
Gallehus gold horn 2	∿	400	(A, no. 23; K, no. 43)
Kalleby stone	∿	400	(A, no. 25; K, no. 61)
Rö stone	⟨, ⟩	400	(A, no. 26; K, no. 73)
Tune stone	⟨, ⟩	400	(A, no. 27, K, no. 72)
Nordhuglo stone	⟨⟩	425	(A, no. 31; K, no. 65)
Tørvika stone	⟩	400-450	(A, no. 32; K, no. 91)
Barmen stone	⟨⟩	400-450	(A, no. 33; K, no. 64)
Stenstad stone	⟨	450	(A, no. 37; K, no. 81)
Kårstad cliff inscription	⟩, ⟨	post 400	(A, no. 40; K, no. 53)
Darum bracteate 5	⟨	450-550	(A, no. 56; K, no. 104)
Skåäng stone	⟨⟩	500	(A, no. 73; K, no. 85)
Vadstena bracteate	⟨	500-550	(A, no. 90; K, no. 2)

4.2. The forms of the runes

Table 7: Forms of the u-rune

(The years indicated are agreed upon by both Antonsen and Krause. Where Krause's dating differs from Antonsen's, it will be noted. All dates are after Christ.)

Øvre Stabu spearhead	ᚾ	150-200	(A, no. 1; K, no. 31)
Himlingøje clasp	ᚾ,ᚾ	200	(A, no. 5; K, no. 10)
Årstad stone	ᚢ	300 (K, mid-6th century)	(A, no. 12; K, no. 58)
Fløksand scraper	ᚾ	350	(A, no. 19; K, no. 37)
Einang stone	ᚾ	350-400	(A, no. 20; K, no. 63)
Opedal stone	ᚢ	350 (K, early 5th century)	(A, no. 21; K, no. 76)
Elgesem stone	ᚾ	450-500	(A, no. 35; K, no. 57)
Kjølevik stone	ᚢ	450 (K, post 500)	(A, no. 38; K, no. 75)
Strøm whetstone	ᚾ	450 (K, 600)	(A, no. 45; K, no. 50)
Fosse bronze plate	ᚾ	450	(A, no. 49; K, no. 48)
Førde fishing weight	ᚾ	450 (K, 550)	(A, no. 51; K, no. 49)
Börringe bracteate	ᚾ,ᚾ,ᚾ	450-550	(A, no. 58; K, no. 110)
Højstrup bracteate	ᚢ	450-550	(A, no. 66; K, no. 116)
Års bracteate	ᚢ	450-550	(A, no. 65; K, no. 108)
Tomstad stone	ᚾ	500	(A, no. 77; K, no. 79)
Sunde stone	ᚾ	500	(A, no. 80; K, no. 90)
Skrydstrup stone	ᚾ,ᚢ	500-550	(A, no. 86; K, no. 109)

teate 1 (see 4.2.2.). This comparison was accomplished much in the same way that a person would compare unclear letters in a handwriting sample with clearer ones. His system analyzes the runes according to the distinctiveness of their component parts: staffs, pockets, branches, and crooks. A staff is defined as a vertical line of full height; pockets as an enclosed space; branches as horizontal or oblique lines; and crooks as bent nonhorizontal lines (Antonsen 1979:288). His definition of crook could be modified to the following: a crook is a bent nonhorizontal line where the interior angle is acute and only one endpoint, if any, may touch the staff.

The features top, center, and bottom are also included in Antonsen's analysis and have to do with the positional relationship of a crook, branch, or pocket to a staff. The feature bottom always implies a redundant top. The terms unilateral and bilateral refer to runes with branches on only one, or both sides of a staff. The rune F *l* is unilateral, and the rune $\mathsf{\uparrow}$ *t* is bilateral.

Kai-Erik Westergaard (1981) employs a very similar system of graphemic analysis, and in fact refers to Antonsen's system (Westergaard 1981:57), but does not exploit Antonsen's analysis. If he had, such statements as some forms of the *r*-rune are difficult to discern from some variants of the *u*-rune, would be unnecessary.

Variations in runes between angular and curved forms will not be discussed because, as Antonsen (1979:288) states, they are not distinctive and these variations can be found in the same inscriptions.

4.2.1. Runic F *f* consists of a staff and two branches which extend upwards from the center of the staff. Distinction from the *a*-rune F is maintained not only in that the branches of the *f*-rune emanate from the center of the staff but also in that the branches point upwards. There are no noteworthy variants.

4.2.2. Runic $\mathsf{\Lambda}$ *u* consists of one staff and one branch which emanates from one end of the staff and proceeds acutely the full length of the staff. Graphic distinction from the *l*-rune F is maintained in that the

4.2. The forms of the runes

endpoint of the *u*-rune's branch extends beyond the midpoint of the staff, e.g. Kylver stone ᚢ *u* and ᛚ *l*; Opedal stone ᚢ *u* and ᛚ *l*; Illerup Ådal shield grip 3 ᚢ *u* and ᛚ *l*. The branch of the *u*-rune may at times show a slight bend which constitutes an obtuse angle: Himlingøje clasp ᚢ and Førde fishing weight ᚢ .

Westergaard (1981:73) has commented that such variants of the *u*-rune are difficult to discern from the *r*-rune ᚱ (see 4.2.5). Graphic distinction, however, is maintained between the *u*-rune and the *r*-rune in that the bend in the branch of the *u*-rune may not cause the branch to proceed back towards the staff: Noleby stone ᚱ *r* and ᚢ *u*; Nebenstedt bracteate 1 ᚱ *r* and ᚢ *u*; Järsberg stone ᚱ *r* and ᚢ *u*; Fyn bracteate 1 ᚱ *r* and ᚢ *u*; Aquincum clasp ᚱ *r* and ᚢ *u*.

The reading of the Fyn bracteate 1 (K, no. 119; A, no. 62; M, 109) provides a noteworthy example of graphemic distinction in the older fuþark. Antonsen (1979:294-5) points out that Noreen first read the proper name on this bracteate as **horaz**, a reading which Bugge at first accepted, but later changed to **houaz**. Since this time, this name has been read as **houaz**. Antonsen (1979) stated that comparison of rune 3 in this name with other indisputable *u*'s shows that this rune is not *u*. My own examination of the inscription in the summer of 1984 also showed Antonsen to be correct. A reading based on Krause's photograph of the Fyn bracteate 1 is difficult, but Moltke's photograph clearly shows the difference between rune 3 of the proper name and the *u*'s of the inscription. In fact, Moltke (1985:109) appears to have painstakingly reproduced the entire inscription correctly below the photograph as ᚣᛁᚹᚱᚺ ᚺᚦᚨᛁᚠᚢᛞᚨᛁᛗᛁᛚᛁᚠ (my underscore) but transliterates them as (R-L) **houaʀ** (L-R) **laþuaaduaaaliia** and ignores the distinction between ᚱ and ᚢ. The distinction between *r* and *u* is exactly paralleled on the Aquincum clasp (see K, Tafel 4, no. 7).

The *u*-rune also has forms which do not appear to consist of one staff and one branch but rather of two branches, e.g. ᚢ on the Årstad stone and the Højstrup bracteate. To be consistent with the definition of staff and branch, we would have to analyze this form as consisting of two branches which do not cross each other. It is an allograph, for there

115

is no doubt that $\bigwedge$ is *u*. A parallel situation may be seen in the Greek alphabet where *u* is either Y or $\bigvee$ (see table 2).

4.2.3. Runic P *þ* consists of one staff and one pocket which is attached to the staff at the staff's center. Graphic distinction is maintained between the *þ*-rune and the *w*-rune in that the pocket of the *w*-rune extends from the top of the staff: Thorsberg chape P *þ* and P *w*; Valsfjord cliff inscription P *þ* and P *w*; Kalleby stone P *þ* and P *w*. At times, however, the *þ*-rune shows forms in which the pocket spans the entire staff: D on the bracteates Fyn 1, Trollhättan, and Skåne 1. As in the case of the *u*-rune, we might be dealing with an allograph since we cannot analyze this variant D as staff plus pocket/ center. The Illerup Ådal shield grips 2 and 3 demonstrate a double-pocketed form, φ (Stoklund 1985, 1986).

4.2.4. Runic F *a* consists of a staff and two branches which deflect downwards. The downward deflection maintains graphic distinction from the *f*-rune Y (see 4.2.1). The *a*-rune also has the form F as on the Højstrup and Körlin bracteates.

4.2.5. Runic R *r* consists of one staff and one branch which has at least one crook in it. Characteristically, no part of the branch, save for the one endpoint where the branch is attached to the staff, touches the staff: Årstad stone R , Strårup neckring R, Kowel spearhead R , Fyn bracteate 1 N (Antonsen 1979; see also 4.2.2), Aquincum clasp N , and Illerup Ådal shield grip 1 R (see Düwel 1981: no. 6, plate 4; Moltke 1985:95).

The *r*-rune N on the Aquincum clasp causes Krause (no. 7) to comment: 'eine ungewöhnliche Form: von der Spitze des Hauptstabes geht zunächst ein gerader Strich nach rechts unten, der sich alsdann in einer nur leicht nach links geneigten Linie nach unten zu fortsetzt, so daß das untere Ende sich der Basis des Stabes wieder etwas nähert; es fehlt also der sonst übliche Fuß'. There is nothing unusual about this *r* if we analyze the *r*-rune as consisting of one staff and at least one crook. If we

116

4.2. The forms of the runes

remember that the crook of the *r*-rune by definition may touch the staff at only one endpoint, then the rune ⟨ᚱ⟩ on the Meldorf fibula may well be read as *r* as proposed by Antonsen (Thompson 1981:15) in his discussion of Klaus Düwel. It is quite obvious from the photograph that the pocket is not closed and therefore eliminates a reading of that rune as *þ* or *w*.

As in the case of the *u*-rune where we have ᚾ and ᚢ (4.2.2), a parallel might be drawn to the case of tailed and tailless *r* ᚱ and ᛈ in the Greek alphabets (see table 2).

4.2.6. Runic ᚲ *k* has two major variants. Characteristically the *k*-rune appears as a crook without a staff and smaller than the other runes in a given inscription: ᚲ on the Barmen stone and Gårdlösa clasp. The Belland stone shows a *k*-rune with full height. Typically the vertex of the crook points to the left or right. Exceptions are ᴠ on the Årstad stone; ᴧ on the Illerup Ådal plane (Moltke/Stoklund 1981), the Börringe bracteate and the Breza marble column.

The *k*-rune also has staffed forms: ᛣ on the Vimose woodplane, the Lindholm bone piece, the Kragehul spearshaft; and ᚤ on the Strøm whetstone, the Järsberg, Ellestad, Stentoften, and Björketorp stones.

It seems curious that the *k*-rune has both staffed and staffless forms. Krause (1966) interprets the staffless forms as the oldest. Moltke (1981:68) suggests that there is a tendency for the staffless runes to acquire a staff. Whether this supposed tendency can be verified or not is doubtful because, of the staffless runes, ᚲ , ᚷ , ᛃ , ᛊ , ◊ , and ᛜ , both ᚷ and ᛜ disappear in the younger runes. The ◊ -rune with a staff (⧫) is a bindrune and represents *ing* (but see ⧫ = *þ*, 4.2.). The *k*-rune and the *j*-rune appear with staffs ᛣ *k*, ᛡ *j* (= A); but the *s*-rune maintains its staffless form ᛋ .

In the case of the *k*-rune, we are again dealing with an allograph. Antonsen (1982:6-7) believes that the form ᚲ (normally of less than full height) is to be explained as a development from the combination of ᛗ and * ᚲ as ᛗᚲ *ek* 'I', which was reanalyzed as ᛗ plus ᚲ (cf. Nordhuglo stone; also see Arntz 1944:42, 81).

4. Runic Epigraphy

4.2.7. Runic X *g* consists of two branches which intersect each other's midpoint. This rune has no noteworthy variants save the form X on the Vimose buckle.

4.2.8. Runic Þ *w* consists of one staff and a pocket placed at the top of the staff. Westergaard (1981:74) states that certain difficulties can arise between reading *w* or *þ*. Although problems may occur, comparison with the *þ*-rune (4.2.3) and also with the *b*-rune ß (but ᛒ on the Gunmarp stone, see 4.2.18) reduce difficulties that may arise. The Illerup shield grips 2 and 3 and the Illerup Ådal spearhead inscriptions show a double-pocketed form of the *w*-rune ᛨ (see Stoklund 1985, 1986).

4.2.9. Runic ᚺ *h* consists of two staffs connected by a horizontal or diagonal line at the center of the two staffs. Variants of this rune are found in continental as well as in English inscriptions where the branch is doubled: ᚺ on the Kylver stone and the Vadstena bracteate, but ᚻ on the Breza column and the Charnay clasp.

4.2.10. Runic ᛏ *n* consists of a staff with one diagonal branch through its center and running downwards ᛏ as on the Øvre Stabu spearhead or upwards ᚠ on the Gallehus gold horn.

4.2.11. Runic | *i* consists of a single staff and requires no further comment.

4.2.12. Runic ᛋ *j* consists of two crooks whose interior angles face each other. The crooks may be arranged vertically: ᛋ on the Thorsberg chape, the Nøvling clasp, and the Stenstad stone, or horizontally: ᛇ on the Øvre Stabu spearhead, the Gallehus gold horn, and the Kalleby stone.

4.2.13. Runic ᛇ *æ* consists of one staff and two bilaterally placed branches on opposite ends of the staff. There are no significant variants.

4.2. The forms of the runes

4.2.14. Runic ᛈ *p* consists of one staff and two unilateral branches placed at opposite ends of the staff. This rune also has the forms ᛗ on the Breza column and ᚹ on the Charnay clasp. The latter may be viewed as the Kylver stone's ᛈ turned on its side where the staff shows a bent line and the branches are straight. It is difficult to draw any conclusions about this rune because it does not appear in any meaningful inscriptions and is attested only sporadically in fuþark inscriptions. The sound /p/ which it designated is also very rare in initial position in Germanic and the rune seems to have fallen out of use and been replaced by the *b*-rune ᛒ as seen in the Vadstena fuþark (Figure 18). The use of the rune ᛈ, however, was continued in England (see Page 1973).

The form ᛗ on the Breza marble column is traditionally interpreted as a variant of ᛈ (K, no. 5; A, no. 104) because this graph occurs in a fuþark in *p*'s place. It is, however, a nonce-form.

4.2.15. Runic ᛋ *s* consists of at least two continuous crooks: ᛋ on the Möjbro, Årstad, and Kylver stones, and on the Lindholm bone piece; or ᛋ on the Strøm whetstone, the Ellestad stone and the Wapno and Sjælland 2 bracteates. The *s*-rune may appear with more than two crooks: ᛋ on the Illerup Ådal shield grip 1 (Düwel 1981), the Thorsberg shieldboss, the Vimose woodplane, the Kragehul spearshaft, the Vetteland, Kalleby, Kylver, Skärkind, and Noleby stones, the Vimose sheathplate, the Næsbjerg clasp, and the Szabadbattyán buckle.

Forms of the *s*-rune with more than three crooks are found on the Himlingøje clasp 1, the Opedal and Krogsta stones, and the Vimose buckle. These allographs of the *s*-rune may represent, as Makaev (1965) has suggested, different schools of runic writing. Again I point out the parallel situation in the archaic Greek and Latin alphabets where *s* has the forms ᛋ or ᛋ or ᛋ (see 2.2 and 3.3).

4.2.16. Runic ᛉ *z* consists of one staff with two bilaterally placed branches which emanate from the center of the staff. Continental inscriptions show the form ᛇ, as on the Charnay clasp.

4. Runic Epigraphy

4.2.17. Runic ↑ *t* consists of one staff and two bilaterally placed branches which proceed downwards from the top of the staff.

4.2.18. Runic ᛒ *b* consists of one branch and two pockets. The pockets are typically joined at the center of the staff: ᛒ on the Nøvling clasp or ᛒ on the Opedal stone. There are also variants of the *b*-rune where the pockets are not connected: ᛒ on the Kylver stone, the Himmelstalund and Kårstad cliff inscriptions, and the Beuchte clasp. The form ᛔ occurs in the drawing of the Gummarp stone and suggests that the top pocket is redundant. Although the original may have had ᛒ , even with the loss of the top pocket, there is no doubt concerning the identification of this rune.

4.2.19. Runic ᛖ *e* consists of two staffs connected by one branch at the top. Westergaard (1981:63) analyzes this rune as two staffs and two branches, ↿ + ↾ . Variant forms of the *e*-rune, such as ∏ on the Illerup Ådal shield grips 2 and 3, the Thorsberg chape, the Gårdlösa clasp, the Vimose woodplane, the Årstad stone, the Nedre Hov scraper, the Opedal stone, and the Strårup neckring, demonstrate that the bent line of ᛖ is merely a variant of the horizontal branch in ∏ .

4.2.20. Runic ᛗ *m* consists of two staffs and two branches, proceeding in opposite directions, which connect the staffs at the top. The *m*-rune has no notable variants.

4.2.21. Runic ↾ *l* consists of one staff and one unilaterally placed branch which proceeds from an endpoint of the staff and does not pass beyond the center of the staff. A variant of the *l*-rune is found in the form ↾ on the Strårup neckring (M, 108), the Fyn 1, Trollhättan, and Ölst bracteates (cf. ᚠ and ᚴ 4.2.4).

4.2.22. Runic ◇ *ñg* consists of a single pocket. A problem which arises with the *ñg*-rune is whether or not we may consider the graph ⬧ as a variant of ◇ (Krause 1966; Moltke 1985; Westergaard 1981) or as a bindrune ᛁ plus ᛜ (Antonsen 1975a). This rune occurs without the staff on the Kylver and Vadstena fuþarks, as well as in the Opedal inscription **birgn͡ggu** (A, no. 21). The form ᛄ always occurs in words with the exception of its occurrence in the Grumpan bracteate fuþark: Tanem stone **mairli͡ngu** (A, no. 81; H, 118): Vimose sheathplate **awi͡ngs** (A, no. 95); Szabadbattyán buckle **mari͡ngs** (A, no. 98; Opitz 1977, no. 43); and Aquincum clasp **ki͡ngia** (A, no. 102; Opitz 1977, no. 1). The form ᛄ, when it stands for the velar nasal, occurs only in inscriptions where *i͡ng* is to be read without any doubt. Whether ᛄ in the Grumpan fuþark should be considered as a mistake or a reanalysis of the *n͡g*-rune must await the discovery of new inscriptions. The bindrune is not to be confused with ᚦ *þ* or ᚹ *w* on Illerup Ådal 2 and 3 (see Stoklund 1985, 1986).

4.2.23. Runic ᛞ *d* consists of two staffs ᛁᛁ joined by two branches which proceed from one end of a staff to the opposite end of another. The form ᛞ on the Vimose chape (A, no. 9) suggests that the distinctiveness from the *m*-rune ᛗ is maintained in that the branches of the *d*-rune are not located at the tops of the staffs. The form ᛞ on the Myklebostad stone is merely ᛞ placed on its side (A, no. 28; H,35-7). The *d*-rune also has the forms ᛞ on the Tørvika stone, the Fyn bracteate 1, and the Valsfjord cliff inscription and ▯ on the Kowel spearhead. This form of the *d*-rune, as Antonsen (1975:9) states, 'can be analyzed, however, as [2 staffs, 2 branches, bottom] (with [top] redundant), so that it can only be *d*'. That the runes ᛞ and ▯ are clearly variants of each other can easily be seen by comparing them to the nondistinctive variants of the *e*-rune, namely ᛖ and ᚢ (see 4.2.19).

4.2.24. Runic ᛟ *o* consists of a pocket with two branches. The forms ᛟ on the Opedal stone (A, no. 21; H, 63) and ᛟ in the Himmelstalund cliff inscriptions (A, no. 44) are to be considered as variants which are turned on their sides (cf. ᛟ Illerup Ådal spearhead).

4.3. The runes and their values

The phonological value of the runes in the older inscriptions (ca. 0-500 A.D.) can be represented as follows (Antonsen 1975a:2):

Obstruents	/p t k/		ᛈ ᛏ ᚲ
	/f þ h/		ᚠ ᚦ ᚺ
	/b d g/		ᛒ ᛞ ᚷ
	/s z/		ᛊ ᛉ
Resonants	/m n l r/		ᛗ ᚾ ᛚ ᚱ
Semivowels	/w j/		ᚹ ᛃ
Vowels	/ī̆/	/ū̆/	ᛁ ᚢ
	/ē̆/	/ō̆/	ᛖ ᛟ
	/ā̆/		ᚨ

There is general agreement among runic scholars concerning these values, except that the rune ᛉ has traditionally been transliterated as 'Nordic' *R* (but see Antonsen 1980a). While Scandinavian runologists as a whole seem loath to give up this 'Nordic' *R*, linguists such as Hans Frede Nielsen (1979:18) accept Antonsen's value /z/, although he keeps the traditional *R* in his transliterations (also Haugen 1982:4, 57-8).

The only consonantal rune not accounted for in the above list is ᛜ, which represents the cluster /ng/ and is therefore superfluous, since this cluster could be rendered by ᚾ ᚷ, as in Reistad **idringaz** (A, no. 41), or by ᚷ alone, as in Svarteborg **igaduz** *Ingaduz* (A, no. 36) and Stenstad **igijon** *Ingijōn* (A, no. 37; see 4.4.1, 4.5). In five inscriptions (4.2.22), this rune appears in the shape ⯁ and represents the cluster /ing/, i.e., it has been combined with the *i*-rune to form a bindrune (contrary to Westergaard 1981:136-79). In Opedal's ᛒᛁᚱᚷᛜᚷᚢ **birgnggu** = *Birgingū* (A, no. 21), the carver has omitted the *i* before *n͡g* and added a superfluous *g* after it. The addition of the extra *g* is undoubtedly an indication of the uncertainty which surrounded the only

4.3. The runes and their values

rune which represented a cluster and is comparable to spelling English [bæŋgor] as *Banggor* (for Bangor, Maine).

There is also general agreement among runic scholars concerning the phonological values of the vocalic runes, except that Krause (1971: 24) assumes that ᚠ can also represent /æ/, which is clearly ruled out by the acrophonic principle for rune-names, since this rune was called *ansuz* (see 4.8).

There remains one vocalic rune which is not represented in the above listing: the 13th rune ᛇ. This rune does not occur in any intelligible inscription from the period before 500 A.D., although it is found in the complete fuþarks from this period. It appears in English runic inscriptions with a strange variety of values. As Page (1973:48) states:

> 'ȝ' [i.e. ᛇ] seems originally to have been a vowel rune, giving a mid-front vowel in the region of *e* or *i*; hence continental runologists sometimes transliterate it *ė* or *ī*. It still is a vowel on the Dover slab, whose inscription '+jȝslhêàrd' records the personal name *Gislheard*. At Thornhill, however, 'ȝ' appears for the palatalized *g* in 'êateȝnne' (the personal name *Eadþegn(e)*), whereas at Great Urswick and Ruthwell it represents the velar and palatal spirants in 'toroȝtedæ' (the personal name *Toroȝtred(æ)* and 'almeȝttig' *(almehtig)*. It is this variety of values that led Dickins to the compromise transliteration 'ȝ'.

The rune ᛇ is also found on the German Freilaubersheim brooch, dated ca. 575 A.D. (K, no. 144), with the value /ī/ in the proper name *Dathina*. In medieval English manuscripts it bears the name *ēoh* or *īh*, while in the St. Gall, Brussels, Trier, and Vatican runica manuscripta, it has the value *k* (Derolez 1954:127). The Anglo-Saxon *Runic Poem* indicates a meaning 'yew-tree'. As Page (1973:79) points out, however, 'The rune does not appear in the later Norse futharks, but the Scandinavian rune-masters attached the cognate name *ȳr* to the rune which represented the sound R ... This may confirm that 'yew-tree' was one of the early rune-names, though we cannot be sure which rune it belonged to'.

The inscriptional and manuscript evidence for the value of this rune is therefore of a secondary and highly suspect nature (cf. the clearly secondary English name and value for the Germanic Ψ -rune: /ks/ and *eohx*, i.e. 'x').

Steblin-Kamenskij (1962) looked into the question of the original value of the rune and came to the conclusion that it was superfluous from the inception of the fuþark, since it was not needed for the phonological system represented in the older inscriptions and there is no basis whatsoever for positing a phoneme between /ī/ and /ē/, as was traditionally done by runologists for this rune (Krause, 1971:26, calls it 'ein sehr geschlossener $\bar{e}$-Laut'). The presence of this rune in the fuþark was therefore an even greater riddle than that of the $\widehat{ng}$-rune.

On the basis of archaic runic spellings with *-ai* for more common *-e* in unstressed syllables, e.g. Möjbro **hahai** and Nøvling **talgidai** (A, nos. 11 and 4), Antonsen (1970, 1986:338) came to the conclusion that runic writing must be considerably older than our extant inscriptions and that it must have arisen at a time when unstressed diphthongs were still present as diphthongs, which would mean that the fuþark was developed to represent the Proto-Germanic phonological system. Unlike the language of the extant inscriptions, which displays a symmetrical system of five short/lax and five long/tense vowels, Proto-Germanic had a skewed system of four vowels in each subsystem:

/ĭ/	/ŭ/		/ī/	/ū/
/ĕ/				
/ă/			/ǣ/	/ō/

Such a system would require no less than six vowel graphemes to represent the necessary contrasts if length/tenseness is disregarded, as in the Mediterranean alphabets: I = /i, ī/, Π = /u, ū/, M = /e/, Ϝ = /a/, Ϙ = /ō/, and therefore ↑ must have represented /ǣ/. It is therefore clear that the rune ↑ was not originally superfluous, although it became so after the rearrangement of the vocalic system in Northwest Germanic, which included the change of /ǣ/ to /ā/ in root syllables and to /ē/ in nonroot syllables. While ↄ thus became superfluous from the point of view of the phonological and graphemic systems of the language, it maintained its place in the fuþark – just as *san* and *qoppa* were retained in Greek – and at a later date in Old English tradition, it was used sporadically in entirely new values.

4.4. Orthographic practices

4.4.1. Nonrepresentation of nasals. The problem of nonrepresentation of nasals in certain environments in runic inscriptions was pointed out by E. Makaev (1965:58-9). He suggested that there were two stages in which this happened: (1) nasal before spirant, e.g. **asugisalas** *ansugīsalᵃs* (Kragehul spearshaft) and (2) nasal before stop, e.g. **ladawarijaʀ** *landawarijaz* (Tørvika stone). The following list contains those words in the older inscriptions which do not designate nasals:

(Group 1)

NwG		OE	OHG	OIc.
uþ	*unþ* (A, no. 105)	ūð-	unzi	unn
asu-	*ansu-* (A, no. 15)	os	Ans	áss
hahai	*hanhē* (A, no. 11)	(hengest)	(Chengisto)	hestr

(Group 2)

lada-	*landa-* (A, no. 15)	land	lant	land
witada-	*witanda-* (A, no. 27)	witend-	wizzent	vitaðr
-mudon	*mundōn* (A, no. 39)	mund	munt	mund
-mudiu	*mundiu* (A, no. 109)	mund	munt	mund
-kudo	*-kundō* (A, no. 46)	-cunde	kunt	-kunda
-hudaz	*-hundaz* (A, no. 5)	hund	hunt	hundr
igijon	*ingijōn* (A, no. 37)	Ing	Ingo	(Yngvi)
igaduz	*ingaduz* (A, no. 36)	---	Inchad	---

Those words, group 3, which designate nasals are: **brando** (A, no. 44), **-gandiz** (A, no. 31), **idringaz** (A, no. 41), **birgn͡ggu** *Birgingū* (A, no. 21), **mairlin͡gu** (A, no. 81), **awin͡gs** (A, no. 95), **marin͡gs** (A, no. 98), and **tantulu** (A, no. 58).

Before proceeding, we should ask ourselves why is it that /n/ is not written in certain environments? If the nondesignation of /n/ is an orthographic practice, then we should ask ourselves what motivated this practice? I believe that we can safely say that the practice was either motivated by a phonological feature, or borrowed.

If the nondesignation of the nasal is caused by a phonological feature, then it can only be that the preceding vowel took on a nasal quality (see Haugen 1982:30). If the vowel is already nasalized, it becomes unnecessary to write the nasal because it is redundant. Since a nasalized vowel phonemically represents a vowel plus a nasal, the alternate spellings in group 3 with the nasals represent the phonemic sequence /VN/: **igijon**, **igaduz** versus **idringaz**; **lada-**, **witada-** versus **brando**, -**gandiz**. These spellings further attest to the phonemic character of the runic writing system.

The nondesignation of the nasal in group 2 could not possibly reflect the loss of /n/. If /n/ were actually lost, we would not expect the spellings with the nasal in group 3. Furthermore, the words in groups 2 and 3 all occur with the nasals in the later languages: Group 3, **brando**, OE *brand*, OHG *brant*, OIc. *brandr;* **gandiz**, OIc. *gandr* and without Verner's law OE *gūð*, OHG *gund-*; for -**ing**- see **igijon**.

While Makaev has suggested that the nondesignation of the nasal in **hahai** and **asu-** (group 1) should be assigned to an earlier stage and held separate from the examples in group 2, there is no evidence in the inscriptions to support this hypothesis. To suggest that the spellings **hahai** and **asu-** preview the later loss of nasals in the Scandinavian and Anglo-Frisian dialects before voiceless fricatives (with compensatory lengthening of the preceding vowel) as a general tendency for Northwest Germanic contradicts evidence from the later dialects. The nasal must still have been present at the time of the inscriptions because it was retained to varying degrees in each of the Germanic languages (see Anton-

4.4. Orthographic practices

sen 1975a:12). OHG *Ans* shows that the nasal was kept; OE *ōs* shows that the nasal must have been retained long enough to cause the change of /a/ to /o/ (see Brunner 1965:36); and in OIc. *áss* the vowel retained nasalization long after the loss of /n/ (Haugen 1982:61).

Since the evidence suggests that the nasals were still present, there is no need to separate this orthographic practice into two stages. The orthographic practice simply shows that nasals need not be written before homorganic consonants.

If this practice were borrowed, then Greek would seem the likely candidate for the lender. Only Greek seems to have had the practice of not writing nssals before consonants (see 2.4), while Latin exhibited this phenomenon only in isolated environments (see 3.6.1). To trace this runic orthographic practice to the Greek practice would then imply an intimate knowledge of Greek epigraphic practice on the part of the original rune-writers.

4.4.2. Double letters. As a rule, double letters are not written in the older runic inscriptions: Dahmsdorf spearhead **ranja** *rannja* (A, no. 7), Kragehul spearshaft **ginu** *ginnu* (A, no. 15, also 119, 120), Stenstad stone **halaz** *hallaz* (A, no. 37, also 45), Darum bracteate 3 **liliz** *lilliz* (A, no. 60), Setre comb. **nanA** *nannā* (A, no. 115), and Berga stone **fino** *finnō* (A, no. 74).

Instances in which double letters are designated are: Reistad stone **unnamz** (A, no. 41), Charnay clasp **iddan** (A, no. 105), Vimose buckle **aadagast, laasauwija** (A, no. 99), and Etelhem clasp **wortaa** (A, no. 110).

The double *n* in *unnāmz* shows that double letters are written when open juncture intervenes: *un-nāmz* 'the untakeable' from PG */un-/ and */nǣm-z/ (cf. also Skodborg **aujaalawin** *auja alawin*, repeated three times and Vetteland **minasstaina** *mīnas staina*). The West Germanic Vimose buckle **aadagast** and **laas-** could show the length of the vowel by doubling but this is unlikely. The second *a* of **aadagast** could be a mistake of ᚠ for ᛏ (A, no. 99). The form **laas-** is the only form which etymologically has a long vowel: **laas-** *lās-*from PG

127

*/lǣs-a-/, OE *lǣs* 'pastureland' and with Verner's law OHG, OS *lāri*, OE *(ge)lǣre* 'empty'. Since this word provides the only instance of a long vowel apparently written with two vowel graphs, it is improbable that the double vowel graph indicates length as in some Latin inscriptions (3.6.2). Taking into account that the first word in this Vimose inscription has a spelling mistake **aadagast** for *andagast*, it seems most reasonable to assume that **laas-** is also spelled incorrectly.

The third case of double vowel graphs in the older inscriptions, namely **wortaa** on the Etelhem clasp is clearly a mistake, especially when the other mistakes in this same inscription are taken into consideration: ᛗ for ᛖ **mkmrlaz** *ek erilaz* (A, no. 110). Furthermore the ending on **wortaa** should be *o* to agree with the first person singular pronoun *ek* 'I', as on the Tune stone **worahto**.

A comparison between runic practice on the one hand, and Latin and Greek on the other, shows that all three regularly wrote single consonants for double ones in their oldest attestations. Latin began writing double consonants at the very end of the 3rd century before Christ (3.6. 2). Even after the practice became regular (ca. 115 B.C.), instances of single consonants for double are still found.

In the matter of Greek practice, we find the same. The oldest inscriptions show single consonants for double ones (ca. 7th and 6th centuries before Christ). Arntz (1944:79), however, incorrectly cited Larfeld (1914:252-5) as saying that the writing of double consonants in Greek inscriptions became the norm for all of Greece by the 5th century before Christ. (Arntz did not state which edition of Larfeld he used. By comparing the pages which Arntz gave, I have concluded that he used the 1914 edition of Larfeld's *Griechische Epigraphik*.) Larfeld (1914:255) qualified his statement that the writing of double consonants became the regular practice in all of Greece by the 5th century before Christ with the following: 'Ausnahmslos ist die Konsonantendoppelung in griechischen Inschriften niemals durchgeführt worden'. Larfeld (1914: Vorwort) further stated that his 1914 edition was not meant to supersede the combined 1898-1902/1907 two volume edition of *Handbuch der griechischen Epigraphik* but rather that it was meant to serve as a condensed

4.5. Bindrunes

version. As the 1914 edition does not contain the same amount of information as the earlier 1902/1907 edition, Larfeld (1914:255) referred the
reader to his 1907 edition (1.269, 2a) for numerous examples of single
consonants written for double consonants. The plentiful exceptions to
the rule that double consonants are written in Greek leads to the conclusion, contrary to Arntz, that Greek vacillated between single and
double consonants.

4.5. Bindrunes

Bindrunes, which may also be called runic ligatures, are found throughout the corpus of the older inscriptions. They consist of a complex of
two or more runes which share a common staff. As in the Greek and
Latin traditions, an important feature in the writing of a ligature is that
each individual part of the ligature retain its graphic integrity. Ligatures
are used to save space and work without causing confusion.

Westergaard (1981:70-72) provides a table of bindrunes as well as
a frequency count. He (1981:47) makes the statement that bindrunes seldom appear in the older inscriptions, which together with his frequency
count, gives the impression that the frequency of occurrence is important. What matters is that they occur in very early runic inscriptions, just
as they do in the Greek and Latin inscriptions (2.6, 3.8). Examples of
bindrunes are as follows:

ᚱᚲ	$\widehat{ek}$	Nordhuglo stone (Antonsen 1982)
ᛗ	$\widehat{em}$	Thorsberg chape (A, no. 2)
ᚱᚢ	$\widehat{eu}$	Opedal stone (A, no. 21)
ᛁᛜ	$\widehat{ing}$	Tanem stone (A, no. 81)
ᛞᚨ	$\widehat{da}$	Tune stone (A, no. 27)
ᚻ	$\widehat{hl}$	Kjølevik stone (A, no. 38)
ᚨᛉ	$\widehat{az}$	Fløksand scraper (A, no. 19)
ᚲᚨ	$\widehat{ka}$	Skåne bracteate 1 (A, no. 85)
ᛗ	$\widehat{emu}$	Kragehul spearshaft (A, no. 15)

129

4. Runic Epigraphy

ᛗᚻ $\widehat{\text{ehw}}$ Skåne bracteate 2 (A, no. 57)
ᛗᚾᚱ $\widehat{\text{eker}}$ Bratsberg clasp (A, no. 75)

Despite the latest attempt by Westergaard (1981:139-79) to treat the runic graph ᛝ, the so-called lantern type of the $\widehat{ng}$-rune, as a variant of ◇ with a staff, the evidence from the inscriptions clearly speaks against his conclusions (see also Odenstedt 1985:3-5). The $\widehat{ng}$-rune is the only rune that can be combined with the *i*-rune so that the *i* can still be seen.

The *i*-rune cannot be combined with any of the staffed runes because it would not be visible. A combination of | with the staffless runes – ᚷ , ᛟ , ᛋ , ᛇ , and ᚲ – would yield another and different rune: ᚷ *g* plus | if combined yield ᛉ which looks like the *z*-rune (4.2.15); or it may yield ᛣ which looks like the *o*-rune (4. 2.24); ᛟ *o* plus | may yield ᛝ̈ which could look like $\widehat{ngz}$; ᛋ *s* plus | may yield ᛒ which could look like a faulty *b*-rune or an upside down *r*-rune; another combination of ᛋ plus | could yield ᛥ which would look like a lopsided *d*-rune (4.2.23); a combination of the *s* allograph ᛢ plus | would yield ᛞ which is *b*; and | plus ᛇ might yield ᛦ which optically looks like more trouble than it is worth. A combination of | plus ᚲ *k* would still be *k* and not *ik*: ᛦ ᛚ * ᚴ (4.2.5). The only rune then which causes no confusion when combined with | is ◇ because there is no other rune that ᛝ can be confused with. If we assume that a principle in making any ligature is that the ligature be recognizable as such in its context and that each element of the ligature is discernible, then ◇ is the only rune with which | can be combined and still be recognizable as | plus ◇ .

Illerup Ådal shield grips 2 and 3 and Illerup Ådal spearheads 1 and 2 now show the form ᛝ which Stoklund (1985, 1986) interprets with the value of *w*. Her interpretation will have far-reaching effects for the reading of this form ᛝ. Her reading of ᛝ as *w*, however, does not alter my analysis here that ᛝ must be treated as a bindrune when it appears with the contextual value of $\widehat{ing}$.

130

4.6. *Direction of writing*

Of 121 interpretable inscriptions (see Appendix A) in the older fuþark, 79 inscriptions contain only one line. Of those 79, 44 inscriptions (8 of them on bracteates) run from left to right and 35 (12 of them on bracteates) run from right to left. The impression made then, is that direction of writing in single-line inscriptions was of no import and was subject to the whim of the rune-writer. In determining the direction of writing on bracteates and other stamped artifacts, I have taken the direction of writing which appears on the finished bracteate, even though the final image contains a mirror image of the stamp. Since the number of interpretable bracteate inscriptions is roughly equal, 8 left-to-right and 12 right-to-left, it will not make much difference in which direction the rune-writer intended his inscription to read.

Of the remaining 42 inscriptions which contain more than one line, 24 (6 of them on bracteates) have multiple lines running in the same direction (6 of them right-to-left) and 18 (5 of them on bracteates) have multiple lines running in different directions. While some of these 18 exhibit a boustrophedon pattern, e.g. the Tune stone, others show the so-called false boustrophedon. For example, the Setre comb bears a three-line inscription, two lines of which occur on side A. The first line is written from left to right, but the second is written from right to left and upside down (Figure 18).

Figure 18: Setre comb, false boustrophedon

The rune-writer probably turned the comb around after having written line 1 and proceeded to write line 2 from left to right. The finished appearance is called false boustrophedon because the rune-writer was actually writing two separate lines, both from left to right.

Arntz (1944:73-6), as well as others (see 1.1.2, 1.2.2, 1.3.2, 1.5.2), makes the assertion that the direction of writing can alternate because many of the runes have identical mirror images, e.g. $\times$, $|$, $\curlyvee$. Other runes, however, seem to face in a fixed direction, e.g. $\digamma$, $\flat$, R . The direction they face in seems to match the general direction of writing. When a rune faces in a direction different from the direction of the other runes, it is referred to as a reversed rune (Ger. *Wenderune,* Da. *venderune*). However, I question whether such a distinction really matters. In the 20th century, where we are used to standardized writing, a reversed letter would stand out blatantly. But just as a child who is learning to write does not seem to care which direction a letter like *s* faces, namely S or ∂ , neither did the rune-writers. Since runic writing could proceed from left-to-right or right-to-left, there was no fixed, 'standardized' direction for the individual runes.

An appropriate point to be made is that runes generally face in the direction in which the line is to be read, but a deviation here and there seems to matter little. A single isolated rune which here and there faces in a direction opposite to the other runes in the same inscription was not significant. A case in point is the carefully planned and executed Gallehus gold horn (cf. K, Abb. 13), where one *h* faces in a different direction from two others: R-3 N , R's 14 and 22 H . If the direction of a single rune were important, or distinctive, one would think that, if anywhere, the Gallehus gold horn would show uniform direction in all of its runes. By the same reasoning, runes turned on their sides or upside-down (Ger. *Sturzrune,* Sw. *stupruna*) are also not significant: Myklebostad Z for M (4.2.23), or Opedal $\bowtie$ for Q (4.2.24; cf. also λ vs. $\curlyvee$, 4.2.6). It does, however, become distinctive when an entire sequence of runes faces in an opposite direction to another whole sequence because the rune-writer is making an attempt to show in which direction the lines should be read.

When more than one line of runes occurs in a given inscription, the second line may (1) run in the same direction as the previous or (2) in a

4.6. Direction of writing

different, opposite direction. The difference of direction becomes optically obvious because they face in another direction. The sequence becomes linguistically distinctive because the order in which the runes are committed to a writing surface is meaningful if read in one direction, but not, if read in the other.

Our premise is then that rune-writers could have taken advantage of ordering in the sequence of runes, namely the direction of writing, to indicate where a new 'sentence' begins. Jeffery (1961:44), as well as Larfeld (1914:305-6), indicates that a change in the boustrophedon pattern of archaic inscriptions was employed as a means of paragraphing. Such a paragraphing device may also be detected in the older runic inscriptions.

The Tune stone inscription (K, no. 72; A, no. 27; H, 109-15; Grønvik 1981), which consists of five lines on two sides of the stone, has long generated dispute among runologists as to which line belongs to which 'sentence'. The inscription, with an interlinear word-by-word translation reads (see Grønvik 1981:259 for picture):

A1	**ek wiwaz after woduri**	→ ↑
	I, Wiwaz, after Woduri-	
A2	**de witadahalaiban worahto**	← ↑
	daz the lord wrought	
B1	**[me]z woduride staina**	← ↑
	for me Woduridaz the stone	
B2	**þrijoz dohtriz dalidun**	→ ↓
	three daughters prepared,	
B3	**arbijarjostez arbijano**	← ↓
	the most legitimate-to-inherit of heirs	

The horizontal arrows indicate in which direction the lines run and the vertical arrows indicate whether the runes stand on their heads (↓) or on their feet (↑).

Ottar Grønvik (1981:123-41) has placed great importance on whether the runes of each succeeding line are head to head or head to

133

foot (i.e. true or false boustrophedon, see 2.5). The interruption of the head-to-foot pattern between lines B1 and B2 signifies, according to Grønvik, a new clause. This system results in the grouping A1, A2, B1 as one 'sentence', and B2 and B3 as the second. This grouping, however, implies that linguistic meaning is connoted by how the letters stand: upside-down or right-side-up. I do not believe that their stance was linguistically or graphically as important as the order in which the runes occurred. The rune-writer may simply have stood on different sides of the stone to write the runes. If he wrote one line from one side right-side-up, and then went to the other side to write a line, which he in all probability wrote right-side-up, the finished product looks like false boustrophedon.

If line A1 goes from left to right and line 2, which clearly belongs with line A1 because the name *Woduridaz* bridges the two lines, runs from right to left, a pattern becomes established in the mind of the reader. The reader then expects the next line to go from left to right, but it does not. He must then stop and begin at the other end of the line to make linguistic sense of the sequence of runes. The break in the pattern, linguistically marked by the verb final position (see Antonsen 1975a; 1981), has the impact of a period. If we group A1 and A2 together, the direction pattern is continuous, left-to-right and right-to-left. If we group B1, B2, and B3 together, we also have an uninterrupted direction pattern: right-to-left, left-to-right, right-to-left.

Such a principle of patterning may also be seen on the Järsberg stone. The main inscription, which is centered on the stone (see Moltke 1981b:82 for picture) is surrounded by another inscription:

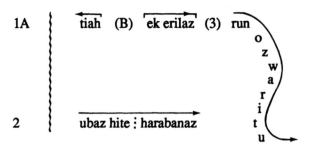

4.6. Direction of writing

Line 1 contains two segments (A) *hait* (R-L) and (B) *ek erilaz* (L-R) which are differentiated by the direction in which they are read. The *hait* and line 3 seem to be a later addition to the inscription because they do not fit in with the symmetry of the main inscription, lines 1b and 2. The person who added lines 1A and 3 may have sought to set off his addendum by having it run in directions different from the main text. A reading which places lines 1 A and B and 3 together, such as Krause's (no. 70), is impossible because the different order in which the runes are read has the same impact as on the Tune stone, namely a period. Furthermore, *ek erilaz ..ubaz hite* 'I, the erilaz, am called [Le]ubaz' (A, no. 48) is a perfectly good formula (cf. Lindholm bone piece, A, no. 17) and *H^{a}rab^{a}naz*, a name set off by dots (cf. Tune stone), is probably the man for whom the stone is erected.

The Eikeland clasp, whose inscription runs around the border of the clasp (see K, no. 17a, Tafel 15), provides another example of paragraphing. The first part of the inscription, **ek wiz wiwio writum runo** 'I, we [i.e. I and my fellows], of the descendants of Wiwaz, wrote the rune [i.e. inscription]' (A, no. 53), runs from left to right. After the last rune of **runo**, the next rune is a bindrune **a͡z**. As this sequence makes no sense initially (i.e. it never represents *za*), the word is read from the opposite direction as *Aisaz* 'the zealous one', a man's name. Perhaps the rune-writer changed direction when he approached this word to make it stand out and not because he had no concept of direction in writing.

Although there are only a few inscriptions in which a type of paragraphing may be seen, a pattern does seem to emerge. When the sequence of linguistic units reflected by the graphic units changes, then the reader must pause. The pause signals to him that an utterance has ended. The Ellestad stone (Marstrander 1952:226-32), whose inscription begins on one side of the stone and continues around the edge to the topside, then swings around to continue in a boustrophedon pattern, shows the continuity of an utterance by its boustrophedon pattern:

135

4. Runic Epigraphy

	←—————————			←—————————
1A	ekA sigim ArAz Afs[A]		(1B)	ka rAisidokA

$$2 \quad \overline{\text{stinA}} \xrightarrow{} \overset{?}{\underset{?}{*z}}$$

$$3 \quad \overline{\text{...kk kiiii kkk...}}$$

The *z at the end of line 2 may indicate that another line ended there because z usually occurs in final position. However, we cannot be sure since the stone is broken. It is impossible to determine the direction in line 3 because it makes no sense to us.

Paragraphing may have been typical for very specialized inscriptions, which the Tune stone seems to be, and not a general rule. It appears that the selection of direction in writing was up to the individual rune-writer, but no direction was standardized until the later younger runes. In the older runes, however, the direction of reading was cued by the direction in which the runes faced.

In comparing the archaic Greek (2.5) and Latin (3.7) traditions with the runic, only Greek exhibits the same features as the runes. In Greek inscriptions, the text may read from left to right, right to left, or boustrophedon. As in the archaic Greek inscriptions, no runic pattern exists to the total exclusion of another, while a certain pattern may predominate in one period. The runic inscriptions in the older fuþark span approximately 500 years and no direction in writing seems to be the exclusively preferred one. There are no examples of the Greek stoichedon pattern in the runic inscriptions, but this absence is not surprising because the stoichedon pattern was a highly stylized form which did not last very long.

The Latin tradition, on the other hand, shows very few examples of anything other than continuous left-to-right writing. Latin has but a few examples of right-to-left and boustrophedon even in the archaic period. The conclusion must be then that runic practice, in this matter, parallels Greek practice.

4.7. Interpunction

4.7. Interpunction

Words in the older runic inscriptions, without exception, were written without spacing, as in the archaic Greek inscriptions, but interpuncts do occur. The use of these interpuncts is limited to dots. Such symbols as ⚘ on the Sjælland bracteate 2, or ˒ on the Skåäng stone never occur within a text and seem to have a purely decorative function. Dots as interpuncts occur either singly ˈ , as on the Kalleby stone (A, no. 25), the Vadstena bracteate (A, no. 90), the Tune stone (A, no. 27), and the Skåne bracteate 1 (A, no. 85); doubly ⦂ , as on the Vimose woodplane (A, no. 10), the Lindholm bone piece (A, no. 17), the Opedal stone (A, no. 21), the Tune stone (A, no. 27), the Reistad stone (A, no. 41), the Noleby stone (A, no. 46), the Börringe bracteate (A, no. 58), the Sjælland bracteate 2 (A, no. 71), the Tomstad stone (A, no. 77), the Vadstena bracteate (A, no. 90), and the Charnay clasp (A, no. 105); triply ⁝ as on the Lindholm bone piece (A, no.17), the Noleby stone (A, no. 46), the Järsberg stone (A, no. 48), the Sjælland bracteate 2 (A, no. 71), and the Tomstad stone (A, no. 77); and in fours ⁞ as on the Vimose woodplane (A, no. 10), the Gallehus gold horn (A, no. 23), and the Garbølle wooden box (A, no. 24).

   Although Arntz (1944:76) is partially correct in stating, 'In Anwendung und Form der Trennungszeichen herrschte von Anfang an große Willkür', he also overstated his position. In all cases where interpuncts are used, they never occur in the middle of a word, be it a simplex or a compound. For example, the Sjælland bracteate 2 inscription reads **hariuhahaitika** ⦂ **farauisa** ⦂ **gibuauja**·⦂·. Interpuncts occur on either side of the compound *farauisa* 'the travel-wise' (A, no. 77; see also Andersen 1970, 1976). The same holds true for ⦂***ekhlewagastiz***⦂ in the Gallehus inscription where almost every word is set off by interpuncts, but the elements of the compound *hlewagastiz* 'protected or famous guest' (A, no. 23) are not interrupted by interpuncts. Furthermore, interpuncts never seem to interrupt I-utterances, i.e. utterances of the type 'I, so and so' or 'I am called', e.g. ⦂ *ek hlewagastiz* ⦂ 'I Hlewagastiz' on the Gallehus gold horn, *e k*

137

wakraz ⫶ 'I, Wakraz' on the Reistad stone, *..ubaz hite* ⫶ '..ubaz am called' on the Järsberg stone, *hariuha haitika* ⫶ *farauisa* ⫶ 'I am called Hariūha' on the Sjælland bracteate 2, and *ek erilaz sawilagaz hateka* ⫶ 'I, the erilaz, am called Sawilagaz'.

The interpuncts also seem to set off or accent phrases which have to do with names. The first interpunct on the Tune stone (A, no. 27; H, 109-15; Grønvik 1981) is a single dot and occurs between *after* and *woduride*, the man for whom the stone was erected. The next set of interpuncts, two dots, occurs after *-halaiban* which is the end of *Wo-duridaz'* cognomen or title. The result is that the phrase · *woduride witadahalaiban* ⫶ is set off by one dot at the beginning and two at the end. The next interpunct, one dot, occurs after *worahto* and probably before a word which ends in *z*. (The stone is broken here but Antonsen and Høst both emend the text with [me]). The next interpunct, two dots, occurs after the name *woduride* again, so that the phrase · *[me]z woduride* ⫶ is set off. Whether the placement of these dots was intentional or coincidental is problematic, and as Arntz (1944:77) suggested, many of the dots may have been erased by weathering. But it seems more than coincidental that these interpuncts, when they do occur, occur preponderantly around names or special words, such as *alu*. Additional examples are Garbølle *hagiradaz⫶tawide* ⫶ 'Hagiradaz made', Kalleby *þrawijan* · *haitinaz was...* 'Þrawija's (monument). (I/he was commanded/called...', Börringe bracteate *tantulu⫶al* 'Tantulū. Magic?', Tomstad stone *...an* ⫶ *waruz* '...a's monument', Charnay ⫶ *uþ faþai* ⫶ ⫶*iddan* ⫶ *liano* 'To (my) husband, Iddo. Liano', and the Vadstena bracteate which shows each family of the fuþark set off with two dots (see Figure 17).

The use of interpuncts in the older runic inscriptions seems to elude any hard and fast rule, since the majority of the inscriptions do not employ them. As Guarducci postulated for the Greek inscriptions (2.7), so the use of interpuncts in the runic inscriptions probably depended largely on the mood of the rune-writer. As in the archaic Greek inscriptions, the use of interpuncts in runic inscriptions is irregular as opposed to Latin inscriptions where most words were regularly separated by a single dot (see 3.10). Furthermore, it is only in Greek inscriptions that any number of dots may be found ·, :, ⋮, ⋮⋮ . In Latin inscriptions, however, the normal usage required only one single dot between words, as Arntz (1944:77) pointed out: 'In den römischen Inschriften wird nur ein einziger Punkt zwischen die Wörter gesetzt'.

4.8. Rune-names

Each of the runes seems to have borne a name which began with the phonological value of that rune. Except for the $\hat{n}g$- and z-runes, sounds which would not occur in initial positions in Proto-Germanic, the acrophonic principle applies. Krause's reconstruction (1948; 1966) of these names as well as his interpretation of them is as follows (cf. Elliott's presentation of the evidence, reproduced in table 8):

ᚠ	*fehu	'cattle, goods'
ᚢ	*ūruz	'aurochs'
ᚦ	*þurisaz	'giant'
ᚠ	*ansuz	'a god'
ᚱ	*raidō	'journey, vehicle'
ᚲ	*kaunan	'sickness'
ᚷ	*gebō	'gift'
ᚹ	*wunjō	'joy'
ᚺ	*haglaz	'hail, i.e. precipitation'
ᚾ	*naudiz	'need'
ᛁ	*īsaz	'ice'
ᛃ	*jēran	'good year'
ᛇ	*īwaz	'yew tree'
ᛈ	*perþō	'a fruit tree?'
ᛉ	*algiz	'elk'
ᛊ	*sōwilō	'sun'
ᛏ	*tīwaz	'a god'
ᛒ	*berkanan	'birch twig'

139

4. Runic Epigraphy

ᛗ	*ehwaz	'horse'
ᛘ	*mannaz	'person'
ᛚ	*laukaz	'leek'
◇	*ingwaz	'a god'
ᛧ	*dagaz	'day'
ᛟ	*ōþalan	'inherited goods'

While the later evidence of the *runica manuscripta* points towards a common Germanic stock for the rune-names (see Derolez 1954; Elliott 1959; Musset 1965; and table 8, below), we cannot be sure that the names of the *runica manuscripta* reflect the original nomenclature. The manuscripts which provide the major sources for the rune-names vary in age from the 9th to the 15th centuries. The 9th-century *Abecedarium Normannicum* (Skt. Gallen MS 878, fol 321), records only the names of the 16 runes in the younger fuþark in a mixed Scandinavian, Anglo-Saxon, and continental Germanic text. The Anglo-Saxon *Runic Poem* (Cotton Otho B 10), a 29-stanza 9th-century mnemonic poem in riddle form provides one of the more detailed accounts of the rune-names. Major portions of the original 9th-century manuscript were destroyed in the 1731 Cotton fire so that the poem survives only through an 18th-century transcription of the original manuscript. The Vienna Codex (National-bibliothek MS 795), a 9th/10th-century manuscript, has a mixture of German and supposed Gothic letters, rather than runes. The Norwegian runic poem contains 16 strophes on the names of the younger runes but is known only from 17th-century copies of a 13th-century (?) manu-script. The Icelandic poem on the younger runes is known from four different manuscripts in the Arnemagnæan collection, the oldest of which dates to the 15th century. Thus, as R.I. Page (1973:75) succinctly states, 'all our rune-names material is comparatively late, giving plenty of time for both English and Norse rune-masters to have tampered with the names of their characters'.

In some cases, the evidence may support a common Germanic form and meaning: OE *feoh*, Abecedarium Normannicum *feu*, OIc., ONorw. *fé*, Go. *fe*, all from PG */fehu/* 'cattle, goods'. The English and

4.8. Rune-names

Norse sources may have identical forms for the rune-names but different meanings: OE *ūr* 'aurochs' or *ūre* 'our', ONorw. *úr* '(iron)slag', OIc. *úr* 'drizzle' (Page 1973:74). Some runes, such as *k*, have a variety of names which makes conjecture on the original Germanic form and meaning academic: OE *cen*'torch?'; OHG *chien, chen, ken* 'torch'; OIc., ONorw. *kaun* 'ulcer'; Abecedarium Normannicum *chaon* '?'; Go. *chozma* '?' (Page 1973:77-8). Some of the evidence from the *runica manuscripta* makes it difficult to determine which name belongs to which rune: ⟨ᛇ⟩ OE *ēoh, ih* 'yew tree', but its ONorw., OIc. cognate *ýr* is applied to the rune ᛦ (Page 1973:79-80; see also 4.3).

In some cases, Krause has taken Scandinavian sources over English because of his belief in the religious nature of the runes: ᚦ OE *þorn* 'thorn' versus ONorw., OIc. *þurs* 'giant'. In the case of the *i*-rune, he has discounted uniform evidence from the *runica manuscripta*: ᛚ OE *lagu* 'lake, water', Abecedarium Normannicum *lagu*, ONorw. *lǫgr*, OIc. *lögr*, Go. *laaz*, which pointed to PG */laguz/* 'water' and substituted the word *laukaz* 'leek', which he connected to fertility rites described in the 14th-century *Vǫlsa þáttr* (Krause 1946:61). He did so on the grounds that Christian teaching would have disapproved of names reflecting pagan rituals.

The names of ᚷ, ᚹ, ᛇ, ᛈ, ᛉ, ᛜ, ᛗ, ᛟ, ᛞ, and ᛝ are not attested in the Scandinavian sources because these runes did not survive into the younger 16-rune fuþark. The result is that reconstructions of their original names must rely on late Old English and questionable Gothic sources. The names of the remaining 16 runes, however, can be compared using English and Scandinavian sources, and as Page (1973:86) states: 'In eleven [cases] the names in the two tongues agree adequately in form and meaning, and for two names *os/óss* and *eoh/ýr*, there is a less clear correspondence. One, *ur*, compares satisfactorily in form but not in meaning. Only two runes, *þorn/þurs* and *cen/kaun*, have distinct names in the two languages'.

The importance of these names lies, for the moment, not so much in what they meant, but in the fact that they all seem to derive from a common source. Furthermore, each of the names begins with the phono-

Table 8: Attested medieval rune-names (Elliott 1959:48-9)

Germanic Runes Names		Old English Runes Names		Abeced. Nord. Runes Names		ON Pr.ON Runes Names		Noreg. Icel Rune Poem	Gothic Runes	Gothic Rune- Letter Names Names		Gothic Letters
ᚠ	*fehu	ᚠ	feoh	ᚡ	feu	ᚠ	*fehu	fé	ᚠ	*fehu	fe	갘
ᚢ	*ūruz	ᚢ	ūr	ᚢ	ūr	ᚢ	*ūruR	úr	ᚢ	*ūrus	urus	각
ᚦ	*þurisaz	ᚦ	þorn	ᚦ	thuris	ᚦ	*þurisaR	þurs	ᚦ	*þūris	thyth	간
ᚨ	*ansuz	ᚨ	ōs	ᚨ	ōs	ᚨ	*ąsuR	óss	ᚨ	*ansus	aza	갂
ᚱ	*raidō	ᚱ	rād	ᚱ	rit	ᚱ	*raiðu	reið	ᚱ	*raida	reda	갓
ᚲ	*kaunaz *kēnaz *kanō	ᚲ	cēn	ᚲ	chaon	ᚲ	*kauna	kaun	ᚲ	*kusma	choroma	갊
ᚷ	*gebō	ᚷ	gyfu						ᚷ	*giba	geuua	갃
ᚹ	*wunjō	ᚹ	wyn						ᚹ	*winja	uuinne	갍
ᚺ	*hagalaz	ᚺ	hægl	ᚺ	hagal	ᚺ	*hagla	hagall hagall	ᚺ	*hagl	haal	갉
ᚾ	*naudiz	ᚾ	nȳd	ᚾ	nauit	ᚾ	*nauðiR	nauðr nauð	ᚾ	*nauþs	noicz	갅
ᛁ	*īsa-	ᛁ	īs	ᛁ	īs	ᛁ	*īsaR	íss	ᛁ	*eis	iiz	갈
ᛃ	*jēra-	ᛃ	gēr	ᛃ	ār	ᛃ	*jāra	ár ár	ᛃ	*jēr	gaar	갌
ᛇ	*eihwaz	ᛇ	ēoh						ᛇ	*aihvus	uuaer	갏
ᛈ	*perþ-	ᛈ	peorð					*þ
perþra	perþra	ᛈ	*pairþra	pertra	감
ᛉ	*algiz	ᛉ	eolh (ecg)	ᛉ	yr	ᛉ	*algiR	yr	ᛉ	*alg	ezec	갆
ᛊ	*sōwulō	ᛊ	sigel	ᛊ	sol	ᛊ	*sōwelu	sól	ᛊ	*sauil	sugil	갋
ᛏ	*teiwaz	ᛏ	tīr	ᛏ	tiu	ᛏ	*tēwaR	týr	ᛏ	*teivs	tyz	갂
ᛒ	*berkan-	ᛒ	beorc	ᛒ	brica	ᛒ	*berkana bjarkan	bjarkan	ᛒ	*bairkan	bercna	가
ᛖ	*ehwaz	ᛖ	eo(h				*ehwaR		ᛖ	*aggis	eyz	갇
ᛗ	*mannaz	ᛗ	man	ᛗ	man	ᛗ	*mannaR	maðr maðr	ᛗ	*manna	manna	갇
ᛚ	*laguz	ᛚ	lagu	ᛚ	lagu	ᛚ	*laguR	lǫgr lǫgr	ᛚ	*lagus	laaz	갎
ᛜ	*inguz	ᛜ	Ing				*ingwaR		ᛜ	*iggvs	eezuz	갗
ᛟ	*ōþila	ᛟ	ēþel			ᛟ	*ōþila	óþila	ᛟ	*ōþal	utal	강
ᛞ	*dagaz	ᛞ	dæg				*dagaR		ᛞ	*dags	daaz	갖

142

logical value of that rune. Exceptions to this are ᛏ, ᚣ, and ◇, the first because its original value (/æ/) was lost, and the latter two because they never occurred in initial position. Whatever the original names of þ and ᚲ, the later manuscript evidence is uniform in having both begin with the sound value of that letter.

These names probably constituted some mnemonic device for learning the runic alphabet, as the Anglo-Saxon *Rune Poem* and the Norwegian and Icelandic parallels indicate (Page 1973:73). What is interesting, however, is that the runes have names like the Greek letters, but not like the Latin: runic *ansuz, *berkanan, *gebō; Gk. *alpha, beta, gamma*; but Latin *a, be, ge*. The names of both the runes, except for n̂g and z, and the Greek letters begin with the sound of that letter. While the Greek letter names did not always mean something (because the Greeks took over the Semitic names), the rune-names did have a meaning, albeit clouded by later traditions and confusion.

4.9. *Epigraphic materials; preparation of the text*

The preparation and execution of a runic text shows striking similarities with the Greek and Latin tradition. First of all, the materials written on are roughly the same in the runic and Mediterranean traditions. People wrote on anything that they could make lines on. Runic inscriptions are found on wood, stone, metal, and bone. They are found on such artifacts as weapons, shields, bracteates, clasps, fibulas, tools, and such personal artifacts as the Setre comb. As yet, no verifiable runic inscriptions have been found on pottery.

The vocabulary of writing in the older runic inscriptions seems to vary, although not to the extent that it does in the younger runes (see Ebel 1963). The root *rūn* itself is related to a series of Indo-European roots */rew-, rw-, rū-/ 'to dig'. NwG *rūn-* means 'written message'. Its etymology reflects the digging, scratching motion of carving runes while its relation to Go. *rūna* 'mystery' and Ger. *raunen* 'whisper' is a case of

143

homonymy with a separate PG */reu-n-, rū-n-/ that meant 'speak (with a raspy voice?)' (see Morris 1985).

The four words used in the inscriptions to designate writing suggest differences in the manner of writing. The verb NwG *wrītana 'to write, scratch' related to Engl. write, Ger. ritzen 'to scratch' (for all etymologies, see Antonsen 1975a), suggests that runes were scratched into a writing material, such as wood, bone, or metal; NwG *faihijana 'to color, paint' suggests that some runes were painted on; NwG *talgijana 'to carve' suggests again that runes were carved into a writing material; and NwG *wurkijana 'to make, create' related to Engl. 'to work (wrought)' suggests that some person was responsible for the creation of the text. Whether this difference in lexical items refers to a division of labor in the making of a text, as it did in the Greek (2.8) and Roman (3.11) traditions, is difficult to determine. However, the different lexemes do seem to imply that originally different modes of writing were used. The verb *faihijana indicates a coloring action and we know that runes on stone were colored at some point in the production process because remnants of the coloring have been found (Moltke 1985:35-6). However, whether the runes were first colored on a stone and then hammered in or viceversa, or whether they were colored in both before and after hammering is difficult to determine. They may also have been copied from a painted Vorlage.

Vocabulary differences in the Greek and Roman traditions (see Susini 1973) may parallel the situation in the runic texts. Lat. scripsit et sculpsit 'wrote and sculpted' may refer to two different activities: scripsit to the person who wrote the inscription, and sculpsit to the person who chiseled the written text into the stone. Gk. ἔγραφε 'wrote' referred to the person who wrote the inscription on an object, while Gk. ἐποίησε 'composed, created' referred to the person who was responsible for the entire operation of making the inscription.

In the case of the Northwest-Germanic vocabulary, the semantic fields of such words as PG */faihijanan/ and */wreitanan/ may have been expanded so that, by the time of Northwest-Germanic, these Proto-Germanic lexemes may have become synonyms. NwG faihidō 'I painted'

144

makes sense on the Vetteland and Einang stone, but NG *fahide* 3rd pers., sg., pret., on the Halskov bracteate does not make sense as 'painted' because bracteates were made from stamps. The use of this verb on bracteates may reflect that the text for the inscription was copied from a painted *Vorlage*.

It would seem that many texts found on stones were first laid out on the stone, perhaps with some coloring agent, before they were incised with a hammer-like tool. While some stone texts, such as Opedal, seem to have been hammered in free hand, i.e. without preliminary arrangement of the text on the stone, others, such as the Järsberg stone and the Noleby stone, seem to have been carefully planned (see 4.6).

The Järsberg inscription has its main text carefully centered on the stone while the additions are added in the margin. The Noleby stone, on the other hand, provides an interesting example of the use of guidelines in the older runic inscriptions. While four lines of text are provided for by the guidelines, only 2 and 1/3 lines are used. In the Greek and Roman tradition, many stones exhibit the same phenomenon. The guidelines were hewn in, but not necessarily used. Arntz's statement (1944:78) that the regular use of guidelines in the older runic inscriptions was improbable, because the edges of the stones or bracteates served as guidelines, seems untenable. The By stone, whose writing surface was artificially hewn (K, no. 71), shows an inscription written along the edge of the stone. The inscription, however, is encased in parallel guidelines. Although the bottom of the longer line of text is worn away, remnants of a guideline are detectable. The shorter line of text, which is not worn, shows both upper and lower guidelines. The Åsum bracteate (K, no. 31) also shows the use of a guideline. I interpret this line as a guideline because it occurs only under the runes. If this line were purely decorative, one would think that it would continue further than the line of text (cf. also K, no. 132 Femø; no. 135 Sønder Rind; 112 Sjælland 1). Stoklund (1985:6) also notes the use of guidelines on the Illerup Ådal spearheads.

Arntz (1944:78) also comments that runes on stones were freestanding and showed no use of guidelines. However, the relative evenness of the runes on the Vånga stone (K, no. 66), the Kalleby stone (K, no. 61), the Rö stone (K, no. 73), and the Berga stone (K, no. 86), for example, suggest that slight guidelines may have been scratched in or colored on, as in Greek and Roman inscriptions. These guidelines then later disappears through weathering.

The Tanem stone inscription (K, no. 89; see Figure 23, below) seems to show a curious use of guidelines. The person who prepared this stone put in undulating, nonparallel guidelines. The execution of the runes attests to the same shaky hand. It seems unlikely that someone would go to the trouble of executing guidelines that are so crooked that they are really of no use. However, it could have been general practice to etch in guidelines for the text, whether these lines were straight or not.

Figure 19: Tanem stone

It seems most likely that when the original rune-writers borrowed the alphabet from a people in the Mediterranean world, they borrowed the technology for working inscriptions. In the Greek and Latin traditions, where epigraphy was an established craft, certain techniques were used in working stone (see 2.8 and 3.11). The writing surface may have been polished to make the surface smoother (as on the By stone). Guidelines were drawn on and sometimes chiseled in (as on the Noleby stone), texts were preliminarily arranged on the stone by means of coloring, and sometimes they were colored in after incising. Texts were also arranged so that names were centered to stand out (as on the Järsberg and Möjbro stones). The situation in the runes may have been such that some technology was borrowed after the runes themselves were borrowed. That is to say that it is quite possible that runic writing on perishable materials preceded the advent of carving in stone by a considerable period of time.

4.10. Types of inscriptions

While the texts of the older runic inscriptions cannot be classified according to the same groupings as in the Roman (3.11) and the Greek (2.10) traditions, certain typological analyses have been done. Lis Jacobsen and Erik Moltke (1942) discuss types of inscriptions (s.v. 'Indskrifttyper'), but their analyses are primarily concerned with the younger runic inscriptions.

Antonsen's (1980b) examination of the typology of the older runic inscriptions, however, has shed some light on interpreting the often terse and obscure texts. He points out by examining the formulas of lengthier inscriptions, such as the Kjølevik stone, that we can infer a formulaic stock for the language of the older runic inscriptions. In the Kjølevik inscription, **hadulaikaz / ek hagustadaz / hlaaiwido magu minino** 'Hadulaikaz. I, Hagusta(l)daz buried my son', the name *Hadulaikaz* stands alone on line 1. Line 2 contains the name of the father *Hagusta(l)daz*. Line 3 explains the relationship of Hagusta(l)daz to Hadulaikaz and what Hagusta(l)daz did: he buried his son and raised the monument.

If this formula, as Antonsen suggests, is applied to the stone inscriptions where only one or two names are mentioned, then we can assume that if only one name is mentioned, it identifies the deceased, the

147

most important piece of information in a dedicatory inscription, and if two are mentioned, then one identifies the deceased and the other the person, probably related to the deceased, who was responsible for raising the stone. If these inscriptions were made or commissioned by members of the upper class, then it would be obvious to the inhabitants of that area who predeceased whom.

Other commemorative inscriptions describe the deceased's station in society. An inscription such as Rosseland **ek wagigaz erilaz agila-mudon** 'I, Wagigaz, the *eril* of Agilamundō' gives the deceased's name in the genitive and indicates the dedicator's relationship to Agilamundō: he was her *eril*. Where the dedicator's name is omitted in such a formula, e.g. Nordhuglo **ek gudija ungandiz** 'I, the priest of Ungandz' it seems that the identification of the deceased, Ungandz, was sufficient to identify the dedicator (Antonsen 1980b:9).

Usually, names appearing alone occur in the nominative case. Occurrences of single names in the genitive are only on stones, e.g. Belland *Keþan* 'Keþa's [stone]'. One might expect that the genitive case, which would indicate ownership might also appear on personal artifacts, such as bracteates, but it does not.

Another group of inscriptions contains words such as *alu* 'ale', *laukaz* 'leek', *ehwu* 'horse', *laþu* 'invitation', *hagalu* 'hail (precipitation)' (see Antonsen 1980b; on *alu*, see Høst 1981). While the cultural significance of these words cannot be determined, it is clear that they carried certain connotations which are lost to us.

An additional group of inscriptions contains fuþarks (see 4.1) and are to be interpreted as a learning, teaching, or decorative device (see Antonsen 1980b: 1, 12 note 3). Such a use of alphabets is also known in the Mediterranean world (see 2.2).

Those names which appear on weapons, such as the Kowel spearhead's *Tilarīds*, should be treated as a separate category. Although these names appear in the nominative case, they do not seem to designate the owner of the weapon but rather the name of the weapon itself (see Düwel 1981).

148

4.10. Types of inscriptions

While it is difficult to draw analogies between what the Germanic peoples wrote about and what their neighbors to the south did – because of cultural differences and the much more limited runic materials – it is interesting to compare the two traditions. The comparison can be based on common human experience. This comparison shows that people wrote about things that were important to them. Consequently, these people wrote about personal topics. The largest group of inscriptions from the ancient world is composed of funerary inscriptions. People, first and foremost, wrote the name of the deceased in a commemorative inscription. As the inscriptions in the Mediterranean world became more elaborate, they began to contain information about the relationships of the deceased (as on the Opedal stone), who erected the inscription (as on the Rö stone), and who wrote the inscription or who was responsible for its creation (as on the Rö and Tune stones).

Other inscriptions which simply contain names in the nominative are also found on loose objects, often personal artifacts, in Greece and Rome. These single names indicate ownership. They could also reflect a donor's name, if the object were a gift. Inscriptions from Greece and Rome often contain references to some deity; the same cannot be said of the runic inscriptions. The only possible reference to a Germanic deity in the older runic inscriptions is the Thorsberg chape's *Wolþuþewaz* 'servant of Ullr'. This name, however, refers to a man, who may have worshipped the god Ullr, and not to the god himself. The common element *ansu-* 'a type of god' in names, e.g. Kragehul *Ansugīsᵃlaz*, Myklebostad *Ansugastiz*, again refers to the person and not the deity. While persons who bore such names may have been intimately involved with religious cults and practices, the mere appearance of their names does not constitute an invocation of the deity. More accurately, these names record a person's existence and secondarily also might attest to the worship of certain gods.

4. Runic Epigraphy

4.11. Conclusion: The origin of the runes?

As no treatise on the origin of the runes would be complete without a specific one-by-one derivation of each rune from its prototype mother alphabet, I am forced to lend myself to this tradition. However, I adhere to this tradition only in the sense that the runes had a mother alphabet. To seek a one-to-one correspondence between a rune and its prototype has been shown by the past 100 years of investigation into this question to be a fruitless endeavor. With each new runic find, our dating of the birth of the runes must be pushed further back in time. Archeologists are constantly reevaluating the chronology of finds not only of northern Europe but of the entire European continent, and hence community. It is a well known fact that amber trade routes existed between the Mediterranean and northern Europe well back into the Bronze Age (see Navarro 1925; Rice 1980). In fact, OE *eolhsand* 'amber' is treated by Schneider (1985) as a borrowing of the Gk. *ēlektrōn/ālektrōn* 'amber' into Germanic. He suggests that this borrowing took place as a result of Greek trading in West Jutland amber during the Bronze Age. Study after study shows the increasing complexity of cultural connections in Bronze-Age Europe while each new archeological find adds another strand to the web of Bronze-Age Europe's cultural interaction (see Schutz 1983). Henrik Thrane (1975:253) summed it up best in his work *Europæiske forbindelser: Bidrag til studiet af fremmede forbindelser i Danmarks yngre broncealder:*

> Vi kan tale om lokal tradition inden for en række genstands-
> typer og traditioner, og påvise typologiske udviklingslinier,
> hvor den stedlige tradition er det væsentlige, men altid vil
> udgangspunktet eller væsentlige ændringer skyldes fremme-
> de forbilleder. Der sker hele tiden en vekselvirkning mellem
> det fremmede og det hjemlige. Nye impulser modtages kon-
> stant, til tider næsten som bølger, der er ved at oversvømme
> landet, men altid absorberes de fremmede elementer og æn-
> dres til noget, der ikke genfindes uden for Norden.

4.11. Conclusion: The origin of the runes?

The interaction between foreign models in northern Europe is also revealed in the respective writing systems. There are too many similarities which demand attention between the runic writing system and the archaic Latin and Greek writing systems.

Before proceeding I should mention that I have not treated the North Italic alphabets in this investigation for several reasons. The first reason is that this has already been done in great detail by Helmut Arntz (1944). Another reason was best stated by Erik Moltke in his discussion of Düwel (Thompson 1981:16): '... in order to create the runes from Etruscan letters the inventor would have had to wander from one Alpine tribe to another, borrowing one rune here and one there'. The third reason, and in my mind by far the most defensible, lies in the language system which the North Italic alphabets represented. We know that Etruscan had no voiced obstruents (see Pfiffig 1969) nor did they possess the sound /o/. The Etruscans did, however, maintain these letters in their alphabet which they obtained from the Greeks, but they did not use them. If they did not have these sounds nor use these letters, then how could they have taught them to the Germanic peoples? Furthermore, if the original rune-writers learned to write from Etruscans, then we would expect some confusion in the designation of voiced and voiceless obstruents in the runic writing system. Such a confusion is nowhere to be found. The only instances where a rune representing a voiced obstruent occurs where the voiceless counterpart should be used are Myklebostad (K, no. 77; A, no. 28) -**gasdiz** and Thorsberg (A, no. 3) **aisgz**. These inscriptions are clearly examples of the neutralization of the voicing contrast after a voiceless fricative.

Moltke (1981a:4) has made the statement that the runes 'were created by people uninterested in phonetic problems'. The creators of the runes may well indeed have been uninterested in phonetic problems – at least consciously – but they were astute enough to adopt and adapt a foreign alphabet which met the needs of their language. Work by Steblin-Kamenskij and Antonsen has constantly demonstrated the phonemic character of the older runic alphabet.

Back in 1898, George Hempl, who was one of Wimmer's first

critics, suggested that the runes came from an archaic Greek alphabet. Isaac Taylor had already suggested this same theory in 1879. This theory was brought back to life in 1966 by Aage Kabell and examined by Antonsen in 1982. If we compare the runes with archaic Greek and Latin alphabets, a striking similarity appears which seems to have been ignored for the past 100 years. Table 9 shows the runes and the letters of the archaic Greek and Latin alphabets. Without the label headings, it might be difficult at first glance to tell which alphabet is which. They all look alike because they ultimately trace their origin to the Greek alphabet. It is rather tedious and fruitless to argue whether runic Ƙ *p* came from Greek or Latin because both Greek and Latin had the same letters; the same is true for most of the runes. Argumentation is deemed necessary, however, where the alphabets diverge.

Latin had no letters for /þ, z, w, j/, which were necessary for the Germanic sound system. Of those four, Greek had letters for two, Ɪ *z* and Ⲅ *w*. If we take the straight cross-bars of Greek *zeta* and break them, e.g. Ӽ , the result is a graph which is identical to the continental *z*-rune Ӽ. Greek *digamma* Ⲅ *w* could easily yield runic Ᵽ if we remember that runes which were carved in wood avoided horizontal lines. Latin *f* and *h* have long been used as arguments against the Greek theory, but Gk. *digamma* could just as easily yield runic Ⱦ *f* as Lat. *f* could. In fact, Lat. *f* comes from Gk. *digamma*. Gk. *heta* could just as easily be the model for runic Ⱨ as Lat. *h* could. In fact, Greek is a better model for runic Ⱨ because Gk. *heta* also had forms with multiple cross-branches as in the continental *h*-rune Ⱨ . The argument used against Gk. *heta* was that it represented the vowel *e*. This was true for the 2nd century after Christ but not of the 5th century before Christ. And who is to say that Gk. *heta* was not continued in certain areas in its value of *h* even after the Milesian spelling reform of 403 B.C.

Various efforts have been made to explain the origin of ◇. Wimmer derived it from Lat. Ϲ . Bugge and von Friesen saw it as a reflection of the Greek practice of writing *gg* to represent *ng*. Marstrander saw it as a reflection of writing *gg* in Celto-Latin practice and considered the English rune ⚔ to be a remnant of this practice: ⚔ is two Ҳ 's placed

4.11. Conclusion: The origin of the runes?

atop each other. Hammarström termed it one of the suppleted runes. Krause (1944:243-7) related it to a supposed old Germanic ideograph. Gerhard Alexander (1975) related this rune to the so-called *agma* (see 2.4) but derived its form from an Etruscan Q. Moltke called it one of the newly created runes. To my knowledge, no one has suggested a relationship between this rune and Gk. *qoppa* Ϙ , which is the ultimate source for Etruscan and Lat. *q*. Although a relationship between runic ◇ *n͡g* and Gk. qoppa [k] is difficult to prove, it is not hard to see. However, the practice of having a special means for representing the cluster *ng* is found in Greek and not in Latin.

If the original rune-writers knew the Greek alphabet well enough, they could have adapted the superfluous letter *qoppa* Ϙ , also Ϙ (see Larfeld 1914:Schriftttafel), to accommodate the sequence /ng/ in Germanic. This rune * Ϙ was then reanalyzed as ◇ plus | , similar to runic * Ͱ (see 4.2.5).

The straight and crooked forms of Gk. *iota* | Ϟ could have been differentiated into two runic graphs, | *i* and Ϟ *j*, and further still to create an additional, necessary vowel rune Ϟ *ǣ*. A form such as runic □ ⊠ *d*, which then developed to Ⴈ, can easily be derived from either Gk. or Lat. *d*. The different shapes of Gk. *rho* Ρ, Ɍ, and D (see Larfeld 1914: Schrifttafel) can be related to the variant *r*-runes, Ɍ and Ρ . The same may be said for the allographs of the *u*-runes: Gk. ∨ and Ⲅ versus runic ∧ and Ⴖ . Latin had only ∨ for *u* and Ɍ for *r*.

While the runes themselves have much in common with both the Greek and Latin letters, they seem to have much more in common with the Greek. The Latin letters demonstrate a much greater uniformity throughout the Roman world than the Greek letters do throughout the Hellenistic world. Aemilius Hübner (1885:LIII-LXVIII), who gives copious notes on the different forms of the Latin letters in the entire Roman world, including those used in Gaul and Germania, indicates that only || *e*, |' *f*, and Đ *d* were used in Gaul and Germania next to the standard Ε, Ϝ , and D of Rome proper.

If we next consider the other aspects of writing in the Roman and

4. Runic Epigraphy

Table 9:

The runes and the archaic Greek and Latin alphabets

Greek		Runes		Latin	
ca. 5th-4th century before Christ				ca. 4th-3rd century before Christ	
Ͱ	w	ፆ	f	ͰΙ*	f
VΥ	u, y	ᚹᚾ	u	V	u, w
⊗	th	ᚦ	þ	---	---
ΔΑ	a	ᚠ	a	ΑΛ	a
ΡΡᗡ	r	ᚱᚾ	r	Ρ	r
Ϙ	k	<ᚴ	k	ΚϜ	k
ᚲ<	g	Χ	g	<G	c (g)
Ͱ	w	ᚹ	w	V	u, w
ΗᚻΗ	h, e	ᚺΗ	h	Η	h
ᛏ	n	ᛏ	n	Ν	n
Ιᛊ	i	Ι	i	Ι	i
Ιᛊ	(j)	ᚼ	j	Ι	(j)
Ιᛊᛁ	i (?)	ᛃ	ǣ	---	---
ᚱ	p	ᛕ	p	ᚱΡ	p
ᛊᛉᛈ	s	ᛊᛉᛈ	s	ᛊᛉᛈ	s
ᛁ	z	Υᚷ	z	---	---
Ţ	t	ᛏ	t	Τ	t
Β	b	Β	b	Β	b
ᛖ	e	ᛗᚾ	e	ͱΙΙ*	e
ᛗ	m	ᛯ	m	Μ𝗪	m
ᚱᛚ	l	ᛚ	l	ᛚᛚ	l
ᛰᛰ	qoppa	◇	ñg	---	---
Δᗡ	d	⬜ᛗᛰ	d	ᚦᗡ*	d
Ω	o	ᛩ	o	Ο⌀	o

* indicates letter form primarily in use in the *limes* area.

154

4.11. Conclusion: The origin of the runes?

Greek worlds, in order to view the whole writing system, we find that the runic tradition corresponds more closely to the Greek tradition than to the Latin.

In Greek, as in the runes, the writing of a nasal before a homorganic obstruent seems to have been optional. In Latin, this occurred optionally only before *s*. The use of double letters in Greek seems to have followed no steadfast rule: double letters could be written or not. While the archaic usage in Latin, where double letters were not written, more closely resembles the runic practice, the original rune-writers could also have generalized a practice of Greek which was optional in Greek. The use of ligatures is attested in both Greek and Latin so that ligatures can be derived from either source. The extensive use of abbreviation in Latin, however, is not attested in the runes.

The flexibility in the direction of writing in the Greek tradition is reflected in the runes. Latin, however, had standardized the direction of left-to-right already in its earlier stages. The system of paragraphing by changing direction in writing within a text is known in both Greek and the runes.

The use and form of interpuncts again matches the Greek system more closely than the Latin. In Greek, words were written without break, whereas in Latin, words were set off from each other either by a single dot or a space.

The rune-names provide an interesting point of comparison in that the Greek letters and the runes have names, but the Latin letters do not: rune-names **fehu, *ūruz;* Gk. *alpha, beta;* but Lat. *a, be.* The original rune-writers could have heard Greek names which did not make any sense to them. Consequently, they made up names which did make sense. Curiously enough, the Greek vowels, *alpha, iota,* and *upsilon* generally designated either short or long vowels. When the runes were first used, ᚠ represented /ă/; ᛁ , /ĭ/; ᚢ , /ŭ/. Gk. *epsilon* after the Milesian writing reform (402 B.C.) designated /ĕ/ while runic ᛗ was originally a short vowel, /ĕ/. Gk. *omicron* O typically designated a short vowel [o] but Gk. *omega* Ωa long/tense vowel [ɔ]. The rune ᛟ originally designated / ɔ /. If a Germanic speaker had heard these two *o-*

155

sounds in Greek, he most likely would have identified his own / ɔ / with Gk. *omega* Ω and not Gk. *omicron* O [o]. While the usage of these vowel graphs in Greek was not consistent in the archaic period, and of course differed from dialect to dialect, an attempt was made through the Milesian writing reform to standardize the graphic-phonological correspondence of the vowel graphs. The similarity between Greek vowels and the runic vowels may of course be a coincidence, if considered by itself, but taken together with other features of Greek epigraphy, it seems to be yet another piece of evidence in favor of a Greek derivation for the runes. Latin exhibited no such features in its use of vowel graphs. In fact, the Romans tried to invent diacritics to designate vowel length. The runes show no such trait.

The last point of comparison lies in the materials used to write on and how this was accomplished. The Roman, Greek, Germanic peoples wrote on almost anything. All three exhibit similarities with each other. The vocabulary in all three languages seems to indicate different processes in the preparation of an inscription for stone. First a rough draft of the text was arranged on the stone and then it was incised. Coloring agents, as well as guidelines, were used in all three traditions. It also seems that one person, a 'foreman', was responsible for the creation of the inscription from beginning to end. The use of wood for daily purposes seems to have been the case in the three traditions although the lack of sufficient quantities of inscriptions on wood (because of its perishable nature) makes it difficult to draw any definite conclusions.

In conclusion, it would seem that the runes came from some Greek tradition. I will not be so bold, however, as to say that I have proven their origin in Greek. Such a proof would be nearly impossible because all the alphabets of Europe derive ultimately from Greek. Consequently, any alphabet tradition will show similarities with the Greek, just as any Indo-European language will show similarities with another because they all ultimately derive from the same source. The origin of the runes cannot be proven on any single aspect of the runic writing tradition. I have described the general features of Greek, Latin and runic epigraphy in an attempt to look at each system as a whole. A comparison based on

156

4.11. Conclusion: The origin of the runes?

any one, single aspect, such as the letters alone, may yield only a coincidental similarity. On appearance alone, the runes could probably be derived from the Semitic alphabet! A series of 'coincidental' similarities, however, no longer comes under the heading of coincidence. These similarities constitute evidence that shows a closer relationship between runic and Greek epigraphy than between Latin and runic epigraphy.

When the runes arose is indeed a difficult question to answer. As older and older inscriptions are found, Antonsen's belief, based on linguistic criteria, that the runes were designed for a stage which predates Northwest-Germanic, namely Proto-Germanic, becomes historically and archeologically more feasible. Moltke (1981a) maintains that some Danish merchant or wealthy landowner, who travelled and had contact with foreign cultures, brought the runes to Scandinavia. Moltke's continuous references, however, to Denmark and Danish merchants is historically unfounded. In fact, it is as erroneous as Grimm's referring to Proto-Germanic as 'urdeutsch' was. If anything, the evidence from Illerup Ådal (see Ilkjær/Lønstrup 1977, 1983) suggests that the Scandinavian tribes were pushing another Germanic tribe (Anglo-Saxon?) out of 'Denmark' around 200 A.D. (cf. Nielsen 1979:14). Furthermore, Lønstrup (1984) now suggests that the Thorsberg finds are war booty from invaders who originated between the Elbe and the Rhein, i.e. non-Scandinavian.

Trade in Jutland amber had been carried on between northern Europe and the Mediterranean, where it was highly valued. The Greeks had established trading posts all over the Mediterranean long before the rise of Rome: Massalia (Marseille) was founded ca. 600 B.C. by the Greeks, and Nicaea (Nice) in the 5th century before Christ by the Massalians. Pytheas of Massalia explored the islands and coast of northern Europe around 350-330 B.C. (Fabricius 1963). In short, it is not difficult to imagine that some Germanic person(s) could have had contact with Greek traders and through this contact, he learned Greek and how to write it and brought this knowledge back with him. From there it spread to the Germanic world.

This treatment of runic and Mediterranean epigraphy, however, has shown that the affinities between the runic tradition, on the one

157

hand, and the archaic Greek and Latin, on the other, exclude the possibility that the runes were borrowed around the birth of Christ from the
Latin tradition – including the Latin tradition in Gaul and Germania – or
from the Greek of that time. By the birth of Christ, these alphabets had
become so stylized that the runes would have had to look more like the
Greek or Latin alphabet of that time to enable us to postulate such a late
borrowing. If the runes were borrowed at that time, the rune-writers
would have written from left to right as was the practice in those days.
They also would have written double letters and probably nasals before
consonants. If they had borrowed the practice of using a special graph to
represent /ng/ from the *limes* area, it should in some way resemble the
graph G , or the more common Roman practice of writing *ng*. One
might also expect, if the runes were borrowed at this time, that there
would be some reflex of the pervasive Roman practice of abbreviating.
But there is none. Roman practice at this time also dictated that words be
separated from one another, but we find no trace of this in the runes.

What about the question of the absence of runic finds in central
Europe in the early centuries of our era? If the Germanic peoples had
learned to write from a Mediterranean people, then we might expect to
find very old runic inscriptions closer to the Mediterranean world. Instead our oldest finds come from northern Europe. The absence of such
finds in central Europe can be attributed to the fact that Germanic
peoples did not settle in this area until the period of the Great Migra-
tions. Prior to this time, intrusions by the Germanic peoples into the
limes area seem to have been primarily of a military nature and short-
lived.

The question of the origin of the runes still remains open to investigation. It has been my goal to show, however, that we cannot use a
priori assumptions that the runes were created around the birth of Christ
to dispose of, or make short shrift, of linguistic evidence which points to
the fact that the runes were designed for a language that predates the
oldest inscriptions.

INDEX OF INSCRIPTIONS TREATED

The letters æ ~ ä, ø ~ ö, and å in Scandinavian names are alphabetized in that order after the letter z. The direction of writing for each inscription is indicated in parentheses: R-L is right-to-left; L-R is left-to-right; M is a multiple line inscription; and O indicates that the lines run in opposite directions. All inscriptions contain one line unless otherwise specified.

B. Mediterranean Inscriptions
(G = Greek; L = Latin)

Index of Inscriptions Treated

BIBLIOGRAPHY

In Scandinavian names, the letters *æ ~ ä, ø ~ ö, å* are alphabetized in that order after *z*. The following abbreviations for periodicals and serials are used:

ABäG = Amsterdamer Beiträge zur älteren Germanistik
AJA   = American Journal of Archaeology
ANF   = Arkiv för nordisk filologi
ANO   = Aarbøger for nordisk Oldkyndighed og Historie
CIL   = Corpus Inscriptionum Latinarum
EG   = Etudes germaniques
JEGP = Journal of English and Germanic Philology
MGS   = Michigan Germanic Studies
MM   = Maal og Minne
NAWG = Nachrichten der Akademie der Wissenschaften in Göttingen, Philologisch-historische Klasse
NJL   = Norwegian Journal of Linguistics
SS   = Scandinavian Studies
ZfDA = Zeitschrift für deutsches Altertum
ZVS   = Zeitschrift für vergleichende Sprachforschung

Agrell, Sigurd. 1927a. *Runornas talmystik och dess antika förebild.* (Skrifter utg. av vetenskapssocieten i Lund, 6) Lund: Gleerup.

Agrell, Sigurd. 1927b. 'Der Ursprung der Runenschrift und die Magie'. *ANF* 43:97-107.

Alexander, Gerhard. 1975. 'Die Herkunft der Ing-Rune'. *ZfDA* 104:1-11.

Andersen, Harry. 1970. 'Runeindskriften på Sjællands-brakteaten 2'. *ANF* 85:180-205.

Andersen, Harry. 1976. 'Til Runeindskriften på Sjællands-brakteaten 2'. *ANF* 92:58-63.

Bibliography

Antonsen, Elmer H. 1963. 'The Proto-Norse vowel system and the younger fuþark'. *SS* 35:195-207.

Antonsen, Elmer H. 1968. Review of *Die Runeninschriften im älteren Fuþark,* by W. Krause, 1966. *Language* 44:627-31.

Antonsen, Elmer H. 1970. 'Toward a new runic grammar'. *The Nordic Languages and Modern Linguistics,* ed. by Hreinn Benediktsson, 313-31. Reykjavík: Vísindafélag Íslendinga.

Antonsen, Elmer H. 1972. 'The Proto-Germanic syllabics (vowels)'. *Toward a grammar of Proto-Germanic,* ed. by Frans von Coetsem, Herbert L. Kufner, 117-40. Tübingen: Niemeyer.

Antonsen, Elmer H. 1975a. *A concise grammar of the older runic inscriptions.* Tübingen: Niemeyer.

Antonsen, Elmer H. 1975b. 'Om nogle sammensatte personnavne i de ældre runeindskrifter'. *NJL* 29:237-46.

Antonsen, Elmer H. 1978. 'On the notion of "archaicizing" inscriptions'. *The Nordic Languages and Modern Linguistics* 3, ed. by John Weinstock, 283-8. Austin: University of Texas Press.

Antonsen, Elmer H. 1979. 'The graphemic system of the Germanic fuþark'. *Essays in honor of Herbert Penzl,* ed. by Irmengard Rauch and Gerald F. Carr, 287-98. (Janua Linguarum. Series maior, 79.) The Hague: Mouton.

Antonsen, Elmer H. 1980a. 'Linguistics and politics in the 19th century: the case of the 15th rune'. *MGS* 6.1:1-16.

Antonsen, Elmer H. 1980b. 'On the typology of the older runic inscriptions'. *SS* 52: 1-15.

Antonsen, Elmer H. 1980c. 'Den ældre fuþark: en gudernes gave eller et hverdagsalfabet?' *MM* 129-43.

Antonsen, Elmer H. 1981. 'On the syntax of the older runic inscriptions'. *MGS* 7:50-61.

Antonsen, Elmer H. 1982. 'Zum Ursprung und Alter des germanischen Fuþarks'. *Festschrift für Karl Schneider,* ed. by Kurt R. Jankowsky and Ernst S. Dick, 3-15. Amsterdam: Benjamins B.V.

Antonsen, Elmer H. 1986. 'Die ältesten Runeninschriften in heutiger Sicht'. *Germanenprobleme in heutiger Sicht,* ed. by Heinrich

Bibliography

Beck, 321-43. Berlin: de Gruyter.

Arntz, Helmut. 1944. *Handbuch der Runenkunde*. Halle/Saale: Max Niemeyer Verlag.

Askeberg, Fritz. 1944. *Norden och kontinenten i gammal tid*. (Studier i forngermanska kulturhistoria.) Uppsala: Almqvist.

Bartoněk, Antonín. 1966. *Development of the long-vowel system in ancient Greek dialects*. Prague: Státní Pedagogické Nakladatelství.

Battle-Huguet, Pedro. 1963. *Epigrafia latina*. 2nd ed. (Filologia Clasica, 2.) Barcelona: Publicaciones de la escuela de filologia de Barcelona.

Beck, Heinrich. 1972. 'Sprachliche Argumente zum Problem des Runenaufkommens'. *ZfDA* 101:1-13.

Benzelius, Ericus. 1724. *Periculum runicum*. Upsaliæ: Wernerianis.

Bergsveinsson, Sveinn. 1971. 'Die Reduktion des nordischen Runenalphabets in sprachhistorischer Sicht'. *Folia Linguistica* 5:388-93.

Bloomfield, Leonard. 1933. *Language*. New York: Henry Holt & Co.

Bohnsack, D. 1967. 'Bernstein und Bernsteinhandel'. *Hoops Reallexikon des germanischen Altertums* 2:288-92. Berlin: de Gruyter.

Bredsdorff, J.H. 1822. 'Om Runeskriftens Oprindelse'. *J.H. Bredsdorffs Udvalgte Afhandlinger*, ed. by Jørgen Glahder (1933). Copenhagen: Munksgaards Forlag.

Brandenstein, W. 1954. *Griechische Sprachwissenschaft 1. Einleitung, Lautsystem, Etymologie*. (Sammlung Göschen, 117.) Berlin: de Gruyter.

Brugmann, Karl. 1900. *Griechische Grammatik*. 3rd ed. (Handbuch der klassischen Altertumswissenschaft, 2.1.) Munich: Beck.

Brøndsted, Johannes. 1940. *Danmarks oldtid*. 4 vols. Copenhagen: Gyldendal.

Brunner, Karl. 1965. *Altenglische Grammatik, nach der angelsächsischen Grammatik von Eduard Sievers*. 3rd rev. ed. Tübingen: Niemeyer.

Bugge, Sophus. 1874. *Om runeskriftens oprindelse*. (Særskilt aftryckt

Bibliography

af Christiana videnskabsselskabs forhandlinger for 1873.) Christiana.

Bugge, Sophus. 1899. *Om runeskriftens begyndelser*. (Beretning om forhandlingerne paa det 5. nordiske filologimøde.) Copenhagen.

Bugge, Sophus 1905-1913. *Runeskriftens Oprindelse og ældste Historie*. Christiana: A.W. Brøggers Bogtrykkeri.

Bugge, Sophus and Magnus Olsen. 1891-1924. *Norges indskrifter med de ældre runer*. Christiana.

Buonamici, Giulio. 1932. *Epigrafia etrusca*. Florence: Rinascimento del libro.

Bundgård, J.A. 1965. 'Why did the art of writing spread to the West? Reflexions on the alphabet of Marsiliana'. *Analecta Romana Instituti Danici* 3:11-72.

Bæksted, Anders. 1943. *Runerne. Deres historie og brug*. Copenhagen: Nyt Nordisk Forlag.

Bæksted, Anders. 1952. *Målruner og troldruner: runemagiske studier*. (Nationalmuseets skrifter. Arkæologisk-historisk række, 4.) Copenhagen: Gyldendal.

Cagnat, René. 1914. *Cours d'épigraphie latine*. Paris: Fontemoing.

Calderini, Aristide. 1974. *Epigrafia*. Turin: Società editrice internazionale.

Carpenter, Rhys. 1933. 'The antiquity of the Greek alphabet'. *AJA* 37:8-29.

Carpenter, Rhys. 1945. 'The alphabet in Italy'. *AJA* 49:452-64.

Conolly, Leo A. 1979. 'The rune ᛋ ᛜ and the Germanic vowel system'. *ABäG* 14:3-32.

Cook, R.M., A.G. Woodhead. 1959. 'The diffusion of the Greek alphabet'. *AJA* 63:175-8.

Corpus Inscriptionum Latinarum. 1918. Volvminis primi pars posterior. Inscriptiones latinae antiqvissimae ad C. Caesaris mortem. Berlin: Georg Reimer.

Derolez, R. 1954. *Runica manuscripta: the English tradition*. (Werke uitgegeven van de faculteit van de wijsbegeerte en letteren.) Brugge: De Tempel.

De Saussure, Ferdinand. 1964. *Cours de linguistique générale*. Paris: Payot.

Dillmann, François-Xavier. 1980. 'Nouvelles études de runologie'. *EG* 35:47-57.

Düwel, Klaus. 1981. 'Runeninschriften auf Waffen'. *Wörter und Sachen im Lichte der Bezeichnungsforschung*, ed. by Ruth Schmidt-Wiegand, 128-67. (Arbeiten zur Frühmittelalterforschung, 1.) Berlin: de Gruyter.

Düwel, Klaus. 1983. *Runenkunde*. 2., um einen Anhang vermehrte Auflage. (Sammlung Metzler, 72.) Stuttgart: Metzler.

Düwel, Klaus. and Michael Gebühr. 1981. 'Die Fibel von Meldorf und die Anfänge der Runenschrift'. *ZfDA* 110:158-75.

Ebel, Else. 1963. *Die Terminologie der Runentechnik*. (Dissertation.) Göttingen.

Elliot, Ralph W.V. 1959. *Runes: an introduction*. Manchester: University Press.

Ernout, A. 1905. 'Le parler de Préneste d'après les inscriptions'. *Mémoires de la Société de Linguistique de Paris* 13:293-349.

Fabricius, E. 1963. 'Pytheas von Massalia'. *Paulys Realencyclopädie der classischen Altertumswissenschaft* 24:314-71. Stuttgart: Druckenmüller.

Friesen, Otto von. 1904. 'Om runskriftens härkomst'. *Språkvetenskapliga sällskapets i Uppsala förhandlingar* 2:1-55.

Friesen, Otto von. 1913. 'Runskriftens härkomst'. *Nordisk tidsskrift for filologi* (serie 4) 1:161-80.

Friesen, Otto von. 1924, *Rö-stenen i Bohuslän och runorna i norden under folkvandringstiden*. (Uppsala Universitets årsskrift. Filosofi, språkvetenskap och historiska vetenskaper, 4.) Uppsala: Lundequist.

Friesen, Otto von. 1931. 'Runornas härkomst'. *ANF* 47:80-133.

Friesen, Otto von. 1933. 'De germanska, anglofrisiska och tyska runorna'. *Nordisk kultur* 6:3-79.

Bibliography

Gelb, Isaac J. 1963. *A study of writing.* Chicago: University of Chicago Press.

Gordon, Arthur E. 1969. *On the origins of the Latin alphabet: Modern views.* (California Studies in Classical Antiquity, 2:157-70.) Berkeley: University of California.

Grenier, A. 1924. 'L'alphabet de Marsiliana et les origines de l'écriture à Rome'. *Mélanges d'archéologie et d'histoire* 41:3-41.

Grønvik, Ottar. 1981. *Runene på Tunesteinen. Alfabet, språkform, budskap.* Oslo: Universitetsforlaget.

Guarducci, Margherita. 1967. *Epigrafia greca.* 4 vols. Rome: Istituto poligrafico dello stato.

Hammarström, Magnus. 1920. 'Beiträge zur Geschichte des etruskischen, lateinischen und griechischen Alphabets'. *Acta Societatis Scientiarum Fennicæ* 49.2:1-58.

Hammarström, Magnus. 1930. 'Om runskriftens härkomst'. *Studier i nordisk filologi* 20:1-65.

Haugen, Einar. 1969. 'On the parsimony of the younger fuþark'. *Festschrift für Konstantin Reichardt,* ed. by Chr. Gellinek, 51-9. Bern: Francke.

Haugen, Einar. 1976. *The Scandinavian languages: An introduction to their history.* Cambridge: Harvard University Press.

Haugen, Einar. 1982. *Scandinavian language structures.* Tübingen: Niemeyer.

Hempl, George. 1899. 'The origin of the runes'. *JEGP* 2:370-74.

Hempl, George. 1902. 'The runes and the Germanic shift'. *JEGP* 4:70-75.

Hübner, Aemilius. 1885. *Exempla scriptvrae epigraphicae latinae a Caesaris dictatoris morte ad aetatem Ivstiniani.* Berlin: Georg Reimer.

Hunger, Ulrich. 1984. *Die Runenkunde im Dritten Reich. Ein Beitrag zur Wissenschafts- und Ideologiegeschichte des Nationalsozialismus.* Bern: Peter Lang.

Høst, Gerd. 1976. *Runer.* Oslo: Aschehoug.

Høst, Gerd. 1981, '"Trylleordet" alu'. *Det norske videnskaps-akademi årbok 1980*, 35-49.

Illkjær, Jørgen and Jørn Lønstrup. 1977. 'Mosefundet fra Illerup ådal'. *Convivium*, 144-68.

Illkjær, Jørgen and Jørn Lønstrup. 1983. 'Der Moorfund im Tal der Illerup Å bei Skanderborg in Ostjütland (Dänemark)'. *Germania* 61:95-116.

Jacobsen, Lis and Erik Moltke. 1941-2. *Danmarks runeindskrifter*. Copenhagen: Munksgaard.

Jeffery, Lillian H. 1961. *The local scripts of archaic Greece*. Oxford: University Press.

Jeffery, Lillian H. 1976. *Archaic Greece: The city-states c. 700-500 B.C.* New York: St. Martin's Press.

Jensen, Hans. 1969. *Sign, symbol and script: an account of man's efforts to write*. 3rd ed. New York: Putnam.

Jensen, Jens Juhl. 1969. 'The problem of the runes in light of some other alphabets'. *NJL* 23:128-46.

Jungandreas, Wolfgang. 1974. 'Die Namen der Runen: Fuþark und Kosmologie'. *Onoma* 18:365-90.

Kabell, Aage. 1967. 'Periculum runicum'. *NJL* 21:94-120.

Kirchhoff, Adolf. 1854. *Das gothische runenalphabet: eine abhandlung. Zweite, durch ein vorwort 'über die entstehung der runenzeichen' vermehrte auflage.* Berlin: Verlag von Wilhelm Hertz.

Klaffenbach, Günther. 1957. *Griechische Epigraphik*. Göttingen: Vandenhoeck & Ruprecht.

Klingenberg, Heinz. 1973. *Runenschrift–Schriftdenken–Runeninschriften*. Heidelberg: Carl Winter.

Krause, Wolfgang. 1944. 'Ing'. *NAWG*, 229-54.

Krause, Wolfgang. 1946-1947. 'Untersuchungen zu den Runennamen I'. *NAWG*, 60-63.

Krause, Wolfgang. 1948. 'Untersuchungen zu den Runennamen II. Runennamen und Götterwelt'. *NAWG*, 93-108.

Krause, Wolfgang. 1966. *Die Runeninschriften im älteren Futhark, mit Beiträgen von Herbert Jankuhn.* (Abhandlungen der Akademie der Wissenschaften in Göttingen Philologisch-historische Klasse,

3. Folge, Nr. 65.) 2 vols. Göttingen: Vandenhoeck & Ruprecht.

Krause, Wolfgang. 1969. 'Die gotische Runeninschrift von Leţcani'. *ZVS* 83:153-61.

Krause, Wolfgang. 1970. *Runen.* (Sammlung Göschen 1244/1244a.) Berlin: de Gruyter.

Krause, Wolfgang. 1971. *Die Sprache der urnordischen Runenschriften.* Heidelberg: Carl Winter.

Larfeld, Wilhelm. 1898-1902. *Handbuch der griechischen Epigraphik.* 2. Band. Die attischen Inschriften. Leipzig: Reisland.

Larfeld, Wilhelm. 1907. *Handbuch der griechischen Epigraphik.* 1. Band. Einleitungs- und Hilfsdisziplinen. Die nicht attischen Inschriften. Leipzig: Reisland.

Larfeld, Wilhelm. 1914. *Griechische Epigraphik.* 3. völlig neubearbeitete Auflage. (Handbuch der klassischen Altertumswissenschaft, vol. 1, pt. 5.) Munich: Beck.

Lehmann, Winfred P. 1977. 'Language and Interference in the Germanic period'. *Sprachliche Interferenz: Festschrift für Werner Betz zum 65. Geburtstag,* ed. by Herbert Kolb and Hartmut Lauffer, 278-91. Tübingen: Niemeyer.

Liestøl, Aslak. 1981. 'The emergence of the Viking runes'. *MGS* 7:107-18.

Limentani, Ida Calabi. 1974. *Epigrafia latina.* 3rd ed. Milan: Cisalpino.

Luft, Wilhelm. 1898. *Studien zu den ältesten germanischen Alphabeten.* Gütersloh: Bertelsmann.

Lønstrup, Jørn. 1984. 'Older and newer theories. The find from Thorsbjerg in light of new discoveries'. *Frühmittelalterliche Studien* 18:91-101.

Makaev, E.A. 1965. *Jazyk drevnejšix runičeskix nadpisej: Lingvističeskij i istoriko-filologičeskij analiz.* Moscow: Nauka.

Marchand, James W. 1959. 'Les Gots ont-ils vraiment connu l'écriture runique?' *Mélanges de linguistique et de philologie. Ferdinand Mossé in Memoriam,* 277-91. Paris: Didier.

Marchand, James W. 1973. *The sounds and phonemes of Wulfila's*

Gothic. (Janua linguarum, series practica, 25.) The Hague: Mouton.

Marquardt, Martha. 1961. *Die Runeninschriften der britischen Inseln*. (Abhandlungen der Akademie der Wissenschaften zu Göttingen, Folge 3, 48.) Göttingen: Vandenhoeck.

Marstrander, Carl J.S. 1928. 'Om runene og runenavnenes oprindelse'. *NJL* 1:85-188.

Marstrander, Carl J.S. 1952. 'De nordiske runeinnskrifter i eldre alfabet. Skrift og språk i folkevandringstiden'. *Viking* 16:1-278.

Meyer, Ernst. 1973. *Einführung in die lateinische Epigraphik*. Darmstadt: Wissenschaftliche Buchgesellschaft.

Moltke, Erik. 1951. 'Er runeskriften opstået i Danmark?'. *Fra nationalmuseets arbejdsmark*, 47-56.

Moltke, Erik. 1976. *Runerne i Danmark og deres oprindelse*. Copenhagen: Forum.

Moltke, Erik. 1981a.'The origin of the runes'. *MGS* 7:3-7.

Moltke, Erik. 1981b. 'Järsbergstenen, en mærkelig värmlandsk runesten'. *Fornvännen* 76:81-90.

Moltke, Erik. 1985. *Runes and their origin. Denmark and elsewhere*. Copenhagen: The National Museum.

Moltke, Erik and Marie Stoklund. 1981. 'Runeindskrifterne fra Illerup mose'. *Kuml*, 67-79.

Morris, Richard L. 1985. 'Northwest-Germanic *rūn-* "rune": A case of homonymy with Go. *rūna* "mystery" '. *Beiträge zur Geschichte der deutschen Sprache und Literatur* 107:344-58.

Müller, Sophus Otto. 1897. *Vor oldtid, Danmarks forhistoriske archæologi almenfattelig fremstillet*. Copenhagen: Det Nordiske Forlag.

Musset, Lucien. 1965. *Introduction à la runologie*. Paris: Aubier Montaigne.

Navarro, J.M. de. 1925. 'Prehistoric routes between northern Europe and Italy defined by the amber trade'. *Geographical Journal* 66:481-507.

Bibliography

Nielsen, Hans Frede. 1979. *De germanske sprog*. Odense: Universitets-
forlag.

Odenstedt, Bengt. 1985. 'Om typologi och grafisk variation i den äldre
futharken. Några reflexioner kring Kai-Erik Westergaards avhand-
ling Skrifttegn og symboler. Noen studier over tegnformer i det
ældre runealfabet'. *ANF* 100:1-15.

Olivier, Revilo P. 1966. 'Apex and sicilicus'. *American Journal of
Philology* 87:129-70.

Opitz, Stephan. 1977. *Südgermanische Runeninschriften im älteren
Futhark aus der Merowingerzeit*. Kirchzarten: Burg-Verlag.

Page, R.I. 1973. *An introduction to English runes*. London: Methuen.

Pedersen, Holger. 1923. 'Runernes oprindelse'. *ANO* 13:35-82.

Penzl, Herbert. 1972. *Methoden der germanischen Linguistik*. Tübingen: Niemeyer.

Pfiffig, Ambros Josef. 1969. *Die etruskische Sprache: Versuch einer
Gesamtdarstellung*. Graz: Akademische Druck- und Verlaganstalt.

Pisani, Vittore. 1957. *Le lingue dell'Italia antica oltre il latino*. Turin:
Rosenberg & Sellier.

Pisani, Vittore. 1966. 'Italische Alphabete und germanische Runen'.
ZVS 80:199-211.

Pittioni, Richard. 1937. 'Zur Frage der Echtheit des Knochenpfriemens
von Maria-Saller-Berg'. *NJL* 8:460-66.

Quak, Arend and K. Samplonius. 1980. 'Eine neue Runeninschrift in den
Niederlanden?'. *ABäG* 15:17-20.

Rice, Patty C. 1980. *Amber: The golden gem of the ages*. New York:
Van Nostrand Reinhold.

Richardson, L.J.D. 1941. 'Agma, a forgotten Greek letter'. *Hermathena*
58:57-69.

Rischel, Jørgen. 1967. *Phoneme, grapheme, and the 'importance' of
distinctions: Functional aspects of the Scandinavian runic reform*.
Stockholm: Research group for quantitative linguistics.

Salin, Bernhard. 1904. *Die altgermanische Thierornamentik*. Stockholm: Beckmans Buchdruckerei.

Sandys, John Edwin. 1969. *Latin epigraphy: An introduction to the study of Latin inscriptions*. Reprint of 1927 ed. Groningen: Bouma's Boekhuis.

Schnall, Uwe. 1973. *Die Runeninschriften des europäischen Kontinents*. (Abhandlungen der Akademie der Wissenschaften in Göttingen, Folge 3, 80.) Göttingen: Vandenhoeck.

Schneider, Karl. 1979. 'Zum gemeingermanischen runischen Schriftsystem (Alter, Runennamen, Struktur der 24er-Reihe, Kimbrische Schöpfung)'. *Integrale Linguistik, Festschrift für Helmut Gipper*, ed. by Edelfraud Bülow, 541-73. Amsterdam: John Benjamins B.V.

Schneider, Karl. 1985. 'Zur Etymologie von ae. *eolhsand* "Bernstein" und *elehtre* "Lupine" im Lichte bronzezeitlichen Handels'. *Collectanea philologica. Festschrift für Helmut Gipper*, ed. by Günter Heintz and Peter Schmitter, 2:669-81. Baden-Baden: Verlag Valentin Koerner.

Schrodt, Richard, 1975. 'Die Eiben-Rune und idg. ei im Germanischen'. *ZfDA* 104:171-9.

Schutz, Herbert. 1983. *The prehistory of Germanic Europe*. New Haven (CT): Yale University Press.

Schwyzer, Eduard. 1939. *Griechische Grammatik*. vol. 1. (Handbuch der Altertumswissenschaft, vol. 2, pt. 1.) Munich: Beck.

Schetelig, Haakon. 1925. *Norges forhistorie: Problemer og resultater i norsk arkæologi*. (Institutet for Sammenlignende Kulturforskning. Serie A: Forelesninger, 5a.) Oslo: Aschehoug.

Spekke, Arnolds. 1957. *The ancient amber routes and the geographical discovery of the eastern Baltic*. Stockholm: M. Goppers.

Steblin-Kamenskij, M.I. 1962. 'Noen fonologiske betraktninger over de eldre runer'. *ANF* 77:1-6.

Stoklund, Marie. 1985. 'De nye runefund fra Illerup ådal og en nyfunden runeindskrift fra Vimose'. *Danske studier*, 5-24.

Stoklund, Marie. 1986. 'Neue Runenfunde in Illerup und Vimose (Ostjütland und Fünen, Dänemark)'. *Germania* 64:75-89.

Sturtevant, Egar H. 1940. *The pronunciation of Greek and Latin*. 2nd ed. Philadelphia: Linguistic Society of America.

Susini, Giancarlo. 1973. *The Roman stonecutter: An introduction to Latin epigraphy*, ed. by E. Badian. Totowa (NJ): Rowman and Littlefield.

Taylor, Isaac. 1879. *Greeks and Goths: A study on the runes*. London: Macmillan.

Thompson, Claiborne W. (ed.) 1981. *Proceedings of the 1st international symposium on runes and runic inscriptions. MGS 7.*

Thrane, Henrik. 1975. *Europæiske forbindelser: Bidrag til studiet af fremmede forbindelser i Danmarks broncealder (periode IV-V).* (Nationalmuseets skrifter: Arkæologisk-historisk række, 16.) Copenhagen: Nationalmuseet.

Thumb, Albert and A. Scherer. 1959. *Handbuch der griechischen Dialekte,* vol. 2. 2nd ed. Heidelberg: Carl Winter.

Traina, Alfonso. 1967. *L'alfabeto e la pronunzia del latino.* 3rd rev. ed. Bologna: Casa editrice patrón.

Trnka, B. 1939. 'Phonological remarks concerning the Scandinavian runic writing'. *Travaux du cercle linguistique de Prague* 8:292-6.

Ullman, B.L. 1927. 'The Etruscan origin of the Roman alphabet and the names of the letters'. *Classical Philology* 22:372-7.

von Friesen (see Friesen).

Warmington, E.H. 1940. *Remains of old Latin.* 4 vols. Cambridge: Harvard University Press.

Westergaard, Kai-Erik. 1981. *Skrifttegn og symboler: Noen studier over tegnformer i det eldre runealfabet.* (Osloer Beiträge zur Germanistik, 6.) Oslo: Germanistisches Institut der Universität Oslo.

Wimmer, Ludvig F.A. 1874. *Runeskriftens oprindelse og udvikling i norden.* Copenhagen: V. Priors Boghandel.

Wimmer, Ludvig F.A. 1887. *Die Runenschrift.* Rev. ed. transl. by F. Holthausen. Berlin: Weidmannsche Buchhandlung.

Worm, Ole. 1651. *Runer, seu Danica literatura, vulgo Gothica dicta luci reddita Opera Olai Wormii D. Medicinæ in Academia Hafniensi Profess. P. Cui accessit de prisca Danorum poesi dissertation.* Editio secunda auctior et locupletior. Hafniæ: M. Martzan.

Bibliography

Woodhead, A.G. 1981. *The study of Greek inscriptions.* 2nd ed. Cambridge: University Press.

Zinn, Ernst. 1950-1951. 'Schlangenschrift'. *Archäologischer Anzeiger. Beiblatt zum Jahrbuch des Archäologischen Instituts* 1:1-36.